confessions of a sinner

jasmine ka wise

Smith family,
I pray that God
speaks to you
through me"
Jasmine

Copyright © 2015 Jasmine Wise

All rights reserved.

ISBN: 1514167875
ISBN-13: 9781514167878

DEDICATION

This book is dedicated to all people that think they have nothing to offer the world. The Lord has filled you with splendor and wonder go share it with others.

CONTENTS

	acknowledgments	i
	introduction	1
1	to look like Christ	7
2	failing others- life of an example	41
3	protection for greatness-guidance	63
4	prayer is powerful	81
5	conclusion	111
6	bible bibliography	113
7	bibliography	114

ACKNOWLEDGMENTS

Many thanks to my mother, Pearl Wise; my adopted brother, Kevin Pranoto; and friend, Jennifer Kluth for reading, critiquing, and correcting my work.

introduction

*If anyone of you lacks wisdom, you should ask God, who
gives generously to all
without finding fault, and it will be given to you.*
James 1:5 NIV

    People that really know me know that writing a book is the last thing on my list of things to do. I hate writing, which is crazy because I am in a doctoral program and will soon have to write a dissertation. I am also terrible at spelling and grammar. (English class was always my worst enemy.) However, the Lord always has plans that are bigger than ours are. He placed the idea for this book while I was driving away from my hometown, Monroe, La, back to graduate school in January of 2014. Praying and driving, I was looking for something more out of my life. After three weeks at home, I realized that my life was somewhat twisted. I was not thriving; not using the talents and gifts the Lord gave me. Sinful places I thought were dead were indeed alive. This is not the way God wanted me to live. I participated in a vision fast, seeking God for a vision, for a path, and to see the how the visions for my life I already had to come to past. I knew that this was what the Lord wanted from me, for me to share my story of failure in self and triumph in Christ.

    Monroe, LA, my hometown, has caused me to sin for some years. When I left for my undergraduate education, I left many doors opened. As one of my close friends texted me, "Ev-ver-REE-time you go to Monroe you act up" (Act up=sin). Every time I go to Monroe, I fell into the roles of whom I once was. As if I did not know God was real. Like I did not know how to love with the love of Christ. I knew it was time for this to stop. It was time to be the transformed me everywhere, not only when it is convenient for me. Therefore, God sent me on a mission, to write this book.

The months leading up to this bright idea from the Lord, God kept reminding me that most of the individuals I encounter think that because I am a Christian that my life is perfect. (Not only me but other Christians.) They believe that I, a follower of Jesus, cannot make the same mistakes that they do. I felt called to write this book to share with others that I am not perfect, but that God's redemption is!

This book has led me to deal with issues that were always on the back burner. It forced me to deal with and gain refreshed freedom. It is a privilege for my God to ask me to write this in His name. This book has four chapters that each tells a piece of my life and how the Lord has triumphed in it.

Chapter 1, to look like Christ, shows how Christ lived and how we, in practical ways, can follow his lead. Jesus Christ is our model and we are called to replicate him. We will not always get it right, but God does not call us to get it right. God calls us to attempt. I pray that in this chapter you see ways that you can begin today living the way Christ did.

Chapter 2 is entitled: Failing Others-Life of an

Example. In this chapter I will tell stories of trying to live a life for Christ and failing within my own strength. Once I sought out the Lord and His strength, it caused me to triumph. You can see triumph in your life as well, if you find your strength in the Lord. I pray that in this chapter you see how God can take what you have done and who you are and cause you to triumph in those areas.

Protection for Greatness-Guidance is chapter three. In this chapter, I share how God has protected and shielded me from certain situations. This is not to say that God does not allow us to go through trials to learn lessons to rely solely on him. I am saying that as his child he wants to protect from the enemy and the traps that he has set up for us. I pray that you see where God has protected you and thank him for these life moments. I also want to you see how you play a part in the protection and placing yourself in a position to be protected.

The last chapter, Prayer is Powerful, shows my road to understanding prayer and what it has done in my life. I know that praying can seem hard and uneventful but the Lord hears the prays of the earnest. My prayer life was and still is a journey to continually seek God in every aspect. I pray that you take some of the lessons that I have learned along the way and apply them to your own prayer life.

Disclaimer: I did not go to seminary. I took only two theology courses in undergrad. I am only writing what I felt led to write by the Holy Spirit. So please ask God what he is saying to you as I share my story.

Dear friends, do not believe everyone who claims to

speak by the Spirit. You must test them to see if the spirit they have comes from God. For there are many false prophets in the world. This is how we know if they have the Spirit of God: If a person claiming to be a prophet[a] acknowledges that Jesus Christ came in a real body, that person has the Spirit of God.
I John 4:1 NLT

Disclaimer #2: This book is truly one of confessions, confessions of whom I once was and whom Christ came to save. I am not perfect. But the God in me is. The purpose of this book is to share what I did and how the Lord redeemed it. My actions are in no way a reflection of my earthly father and mother but rather my own sinful, fleshy, nature. The battle does not rest in the hands of someone else but ourselves.

And if you do not carry your own cross and follow me, you cannot be my disciple.
Luke 14:27 NLT

This book and my writing style are both conversational in nature. I want to attribute this to the Apostle Paul. If you look at many of his writings he talks about the bad in him, church, or other group of people then there will be a "but." But God is real. But God saves. But God cares for you. As I tell my story, you will see many "buts"; they are not mistakes. They are realizations that God has saved me and taken what I once was and made me who I am today: a soul that longs to be near Him and look like His Son.

I pray that at the end of this book you will examine your own life. I pray that you imagine your own story and see how God has and can use you despite the sins and mistakes and despite what you believe about yourself.

We are His children and He wants us to live a fulfilling life dedicated to Him!

I pray you enjoy my story and are able to learn and grow from it.

1 to look like Christ

I prayed for years and years "Lord, let people see you when they see me." This prayer was answered when a man I just met told me I shined like Christ. That is the biggest compliment that anyone could ever receive.

Therefore be imitators of God, as beloved children. And walk in love, as Christ loved us and gave himself up for us, a fragrant offering and sacrifice to God.
Ephesians 5:1-2 ESV

On a Saturday afternoon in January of 2014, my mother and I were walking down the street telling members of the community to come visit my home church in Monroe, LA. A lot was changing: service times, new choir members, and additional volunteers to fill in some things we had been missing. I knew it was going to be amazing. About halfway down South 7th street as we are crossing a main road in the neighborhood I looked at her and said, "I never want to look like a Christian." She looked at me with the widest eyes I have ever gotten from her. Later that night I explained more. Christians have a bad reputation in our society so I do not want to be associated. I want to be associated with Jesus Christ.

I have been saying similar things for years. Every time I say this or a statement similar, an older member of my church looks at me as if I am clearly on the wrong path. As a young Christian, I must have lost myself not to want to look like a Christian.

Actually, the contrary is true. I have found myself and realized that I want to look like Christ in every aspect of my life, not just a Christian. I finally realized that this is what I am called to do. When I first decided to follow the Lord with my whole being about six years before this encounter with my mother, I worked very hard to look like a Christian. I always said the right things, went to the right functions, and worked in the right ministries. I was so silly, I even judged my other Christian friends for not looking like me. I find myself now still battling with what we are "supposed" to say, do, and even think. Now do not get me wrong, we will be held accountable for our sins and there are duties like praying and reading the bible. But what about regular church attendance? Or being a part of the choir if everyone in the church knows you can sing? Or having tattoos and piercings? Do these things make us any more or less Christian?

Are you practicing?

I met a young man at a conference about five years ago that was Muslim. After he shared this piece of information with me, he quickly added that he was not a "practicing Muslim." He meant that he identified with the religion but was not currently following the teachings of the Koran. He was not abiding by the creed, traditions, or rituals of the faith. To be a member of any religious faith one must first know the teachings of that faith and secondly practice those teachings.

This encounter stayed with me for two reasons. First, he was so honest with me about his religious status. Not that he was Muslim, but that he was not practicing and participating in the religious teachings. Secondly, because there are so many people that claim to be Christians but are not practicing the faith.

If more people were honest with themselves and others, the Christian faith would not get such a bad rap. This would mean we would have to be more real with ourselves. We would have to admit that we are not chasing after God. It is a hard thing to do. Not many people want to admit that they are not following the religion that they claim to believe in with all of their heart.

Where I grew up, Christianity is the default religion. I have people in my life that say they are Christian but absolutely nothing in their lives resemble Him. There is no bible found and they laugh when I say, "let's pray about it." Some of us are quick to tell people that we are Christian but do not live the lifestyle of Christ.

Coming from a highly religious church, where traditions and rules abound, it is sometimes hard for me to listen to the Holy Spirit and do what he says because I am so used to having a set of rules to follow. I was used to following the magic formula to achieve righteousness and holiness. Looking like Christ means loving others without judgment. It's giving until the Lord tells you to stop. It's serving. It's lowering yourself so that others can rise above you. It's not getting offended easily.

Changes in Scenery

Transforming from non-practicing to practicing

follower of Christ was not a physical change, but a heart change for me. While I surrendered my heart to Him, God was faithful to continually mold me. Moving to Waco, TX was one the best decisions that Lord has made for me. The Lord knew in order for me to grow in the faith and have new revelations in Him I must be alone. Surrounded by people that did not know my personally. When I left for college, although growing in my faith, I moved to New Orleans, LA. In New Orleans, I had close family members and a branch of my church filled with individuals that have known me since I was young. So again, I fell into the same roles, somebody's daughter, niece, or sister. I did not have a chance to define myself and continued to live the same empty life trying to please others instead of God.

Moving to Waco was an opportunity for me to meet new people. I explored new options and defined myself based on who I was, not who people defined me to be. My church in Waco was so different from my hometown church that I grew in faith and redefined what church and my relationship with Christ looked like. I can truly say that I learned more about the Lord and myself as an individual more in the year and a half being in Waco than I had at any other time in my life. This is not to say my home church did not teach me. It is that new things cause you to question what you believe and why. I decided on my own that most of the things I was taught were right but I believe more strongly because I had to walk them out on my own.

At my Waco home church, I remember a woman was dancing near me with a flag in worship to the Lord and she almost hit me! That would have never happened at my old church. The most people do is raise their hands (which is not a lesser than form of worship at all). It was amazing to see people worship in a different way. There are even people that openly dance unto the Lord. As a new comer to this church, I had no idea where to place these people in my well-defined ways of worship. They did not fit my list.

One of the first things I realized about my new church was their emphasis on showing others Christ through words and actions.

I was for the first time commissioned to share my faith with others. As I began to share what I believe with others, I realized that some people did not want to hear what I had to say. I wore so proudly the banner of Christianity but was continually knocked down by it. Soon the Lord opened my eyes. He showed me through relationships with others that there is no one way to look to the outside world but one way to be: a follower of Christ.

This church is where I truly saw the meaning of the common phrase, "come as you are." We have every type person attend our church: young, old, wealthy, poor, Black, Caucasian, Asian, Hispanic, professors, janitors, college students, bikers, homeless people, everyone! How could I say that a Christian must look one way when all of these people profess to know the Lord? It is impossible.

I knew that I wanted to look like Christ but that was it. I had no clue what Christ looked like. At that time in my life, I decided to reread the books of the bible called the Gospels: Matthew, Mark, Luke, and John. In order to live like Christ, I needed to know what He did. This was the best way I knew to learn.

What did Christ do?

Christ loved all. Christ died for us all.

By this we know love, that he laid down His life for us, and we ought to lay down our lives for the brothers.
1 John 3:16 ESV

The ultimate calling on Christ's life was to love us purely enough to give His life up for us. To be completely honest, the only people I am willing to give up life for are my grandmother and my parents. I cannot imagine giving up my life for people that have not been born yet. I cannot imagine giving up my life for the people that were going to kill me. But Christ did it because he loved us.

Love is patient and kind; love does not envy or boast; it is not arrogant or rude. It does not insist on its own way; it is not irritable or resentful; it does not rejoice at wrongdoing, but rejoices with the truth. Love bears all things, believes all things, hopes all things, endures all things. Love never ends. As for prophecies, they will pass away; as for tongues, they will cease; as for knowledge, it will pass away. For we know in part and we prophesy in part, but when the perfect comes, the partial will pass away.
1 Corinthians 13:4-10 ESV

Wedding officiates speak these verses often as a reminder to the married people to love each other purely and that it will change any situation in the marriage. These verses are not just for married individuals. They are a reminder of how to treat others, all people, not just the people that I like with pure love. If I am being resentful, I know that I am not being loving and therefore not being like Christ. If I keep count of wrong doings, I am not being like Christ. If I am being selfish, I am not being like Christ. I now know that I must put myself to the side, or die, in order to love in all ways.

I know when I am being selfish most when I "forget" things. I used to "forget" birthday parties, to return phone calls, and study groups. During undergrad, I was "forgetting" a lot of events and people. I never truly forgot any of those people, I just did want to go to the event or hang out with that person. I know that not wanting to hang out with a group of friends is not bad, but acting as if you do and then not doing it is an act of selfishness. Gladly, if anyone noticed my selfishness they never called me out on it. I now know that being honest is less selfish and more open.

I now know that "forgetting" is not of the Lord and is my selfish nature. Instead, I choose now to be selfless; this is what Christ did for us and this is what I strive to do for those around me.

How do I love?

At the church I currently attend, I work with the youth. They are truly my people. I see them at least once a week and truly believe that they are all my little brothers and sisters. They have all taught me lessons about faith and looking like Jesus. Although we have respectful youth that are morally good people, I am more interested in the underneath. The ugly things inside of us cause us to stumble. The youth, like the rest of us as a church, have issues and obstacles. I have had to learn to love like Jesus. Ministry is hard and youth are stubborn, but the Lord reminds me that I too am stubborn and His ministry was harder.

I can truly say that I have learned more and more through my experiences with the youth how to love purely, how to share what God has given me. I attempt to be as selfless as possible with the youth and show them that I have their backs. It crazy to see brokenness and hurt in a 14-year-olds eyes who has been hurt by divorce, sex, homelessness, and much more. Some of the youth are so uncomfortable with themselves they barely look at me when I talk to them. Some of them have been in worse situations than I could have dreamed up. But Christ's love, crucifixion, and resurrection can fix all of it. I want them to know this.

As I minister to them, they grow me. They give me more and more opportunities to love, to look like Christ, to see the church lived out.

I also have had to learn how to die to my flesh. There are many times when I want to tell the youth to "just get over it" when they complain about a failing relationship or that "it's not the end of the world" when their soccer team loses. I cannot do that. The Lord is longsuffering with me enough to die for me so I can do the same with the youth.

I now see that the youth also have to be longsuffering with me. I know that there are days that I get on their nerves or ask them too many questions about their lives, but somehow they still love me.

Being a youth leader has truly changed how I see Christ and the love he has for us.

"I have loved you even as the Father has loved me. Remain in my love. When you obey my commandments, you remain in my love, just as I obey my Father's commandments and remain in his love. I have told you these things so that you will be filled with my joy. Yes, your joy will overflow! This is my commandment: Love each other in the same way I have loved you."
John 15:9-12 NLT

In the above scripture, Jesus is talking to the disciples about his relationship to the Father and to them. There have been times where I have to remind myself of the scripture above and what it really says. In my extreme paraphrasing, Jesus is telling the disciples to love one another the same way he loves them, which is the same way God loves Jesus. That is a lot of love; a whole lot of love. No one can measure the amount of love God has for Jesus, or that Jesus has for us, but that is how much love we are to have for others.

There are many times when I ask God what to do with a friend that bails on me continually or a coworker that does not seem to understand me at all. God's response is always the same: "Love them." Many times I ask God, "Why me?" Why do I have to love unconditionally while the other person can continue to act with little or no love toward me? I know that God wants me to look like him in every situation. If God can forgive me of my sins towards him, I can forgive a flaky friend.

After this, I started asking, "What does it mean to love them?" I soon realized that in most of these situations it meant forgiveness and patience. Both are acts of love that God gives to us daily.

Christ built relationships and discipled others

One of my favorite stories in the bible is when Jesus fed the 5,000+ people in a field and preached to them.

So Jesus and his followers went away alone. They went in a boat to a place where no one lived. But many people saw them leave and knew who they were. So people from every town ran to the place where they were going and got there before Jesus. As Jesus stepped out of the boat, he saw a large crowd waiting. He felt sorry for them, because they were like sheep without a shepherd to care for them. So he taught the people many things. It was now very late in the day. Jesus' followers came to him and said, "No one lives around here, and it is already very late. So send the people away. They need to go to the farms and towns around here to buy some food to eat."
But Jesus answered, "You give them some food to eat."
Mark 6:32-37a ERV

This is my favorite story because it is a clear example of holistic ministry led by Jesus. Jesus fed the people spiritually and then he and his disciples met their physical needs of hunger. I believe that praying for a starving man on the street corner to get food when it is within our ability to answer that prayer, is not showing the love of Christ. Instead, we could be harming our testimony. If that starving man knows that you have plenty and can give to Him, but you continually tell Him about Jesus without sharing bread with him, it may be hard for Him to receive what you are saying at that moment. We must do as the disciples did and give others food to eat. The people we talk to about God must be open to hear our message. This is harder to do if their basic needs go unmet. I do believe that there are situations when it may be more harmful to provide aid than it would be to empower someone to provide for him or herself, but some of us have not even started giving to others to begin with. The word of God says that we should turn no one away when we asked to help.

Give to those who ask, and don't turn away from those who want to borrow. Matthew 5:42 NLT

Whoever is kind to the poor lends to the LORD, and he will reward them for what they have done. Proverbs 19:17 NIV

The generous will prosper; those who refresh others will themselves be refreshed. Proverbs 11:25 NLT

In my short time working with families, I see that people are not very interested in hearing the Gospel when I have no credibility with them. I have not built a relationship with them or even learned their names. We, as the hands and feet of Christ, have to meet people's needs spiritual and physical. If the people we are telling the Good News of Christ to or even holding a conversation with do not come to our churches that Sunday or receive Christ at the moment, it is okay. We have planted a seed of kindness, one of the fruits we are to always bear. It is more blessed to give than to receive anyways.

… You should remember the words of the Lord Jesus: 'It is more blessed to give than to receive.'
Acts 20:35b NLT

Jesus was continually blessing people. No matter where he was, he gave to others. Jesus blessed despite not having the comforts that most people today use as measures of success, like a home.

Jesus replied, "Foxes have dens and birds have nests, but the Son of Man has no place to lay his head."
Luke 9:58 NIV

When we build relationships, we build accountably with others. I am so thankful for the people in my life who keep me accountable. Yes, we are here to share the Gospel and bring others to Christ, but we are also to build relationships so that people know what to do after they receive Christ. We are here to show through our actions how Jesus lived and how he scarified for us. We are to open our homes and allow others to feel safe, similar to what they will find in Jesus. Think about the ministry Christ led. He kept the disciples accountable in all their ways.

He consistently asked questions about their faith and sometimes humbled them. Christ built close relationships with these twelve men; he lived, traveled, ate, and most importantly ministered with them to show the way. He discipled these men so that they could go out and disciple others. In Matthew 17 Jesus asked the disciples, "How long must I be with you?" after they could not cast a demon out a boy. He asks them this because he wants them to understand that he will not be there long with them but also that they might have faith to do wonders on their own.

There was a lesson in everything Jesus did with the

disciples. He wanted them to see and know that they had power. The same power that he had from God, they possessed too. This passage shows me that even those who lived with Christ day in and day out failed at times. It further proves that Jesus was perfect and we will all fall short. But with guidance, wisdom, and grace we can grow and learn from God.

We are all called to a life of discipleship. Discipleship is simply committing to learn from someone further along in his or her relationship with Jesus than you and to grow, with the help of the Lord, in your relationship with Jesus. Once we receive Christ, we have knowledge of truth. This knowledge is valuable to all people. As we decide to live alongside others and share the knowledge of the truth that we have, we are involving ourselves in discipleship. I now know that I am not to rely on others for my strength, but I am to receive guidance when I need it from them.

As iron sharpens iron, so a friend sharpens a friend.
Proverbs 27:17 NLT

At one point in my life, I had a situation with a guy that I thought I desperately needed to talk with my discipler. I felt like I was in crisis. But she could not meet with me until the following week. I was not upset with her; I understood that she had a family and obligations. I still felt like I needed to tell her so she could fix it and be my strength. God showed me that I am to always go to him first; my strength comes from him. After I went to God, I was actually able to better communicate with my discipler in a way that I would not have been able to before I talked to God. In that situation, God was showing me that I was relying on the Christian community that he has blessed me with more that I was on him.

My mother and my discipler at the time kept me accountable the most. I learned through them that it is okay to fall down and slip up, but it is not okay to stay down. They are both straightforward women and will keep me on my toes. I need them, but I know that I would not receive this type of treatment from people I do not have a close or any type of relationship with. Again, I believe that relationships are key to change any person to love and follow Christ.

My home church has a slogan that says "Each one, Reach one." We are all called to change at least one person. We are not all called to do short term missions or go to a different country to live for three years. However, we are all a part of a community, a community where the Lord has placed us. Find one person and build a relationship with them. That is one way to grow the Kingdom. Jesus reached masses of people, but the life-lasting change occurred in the one-on-one encounters and discipleship.

Christ was a servant

Jesus washed the feet of the disciples. In that time, washing feet was a task for servants or those lower on the societal ladder. Jesus wanted to show the world that he was here to serve others, not to be served. We should do the same for others around us. We should serve them in ways that the world will not understand. There is a ministry in Waco, TX that washes the feet of the homeless and gives them fresh socks around Easter.

This is who God wants us to be. He calls us to do uncomfortable things that will benefit others. This is the mark of a true servant in my eyes.

We are to "wash the feet" of those around us. We are to serve them. We have to look past ourselves and see how others will be changed if we serve them. Serving looks different for different people. My personal motto when it comes to serving is, "If you see a need, meet it." I believe that God does not allow me to see the need if he does not want me to meet it in some way. If I see that a child has a hard time in school and needs a tutor, I may not be able to tutor them but I can find a college student who is willing to do so. That is still meeting the need of that child. We all must put our best foot forward in being a servant.

When Jesus noticed that all who had come to the dinner were trying to sit in the seats of honor near the head of the table, he gave them this advice: "When you are invited to a wedding feast, don't sit in the seat of honor. What if someone who is more distinguished than you has also been invited? The host will come and say, 'Give this person your seat.' Then you will be embarrassed, and you will have to take whatever seat is left at the foot of the table!
… For those who exalt themselves will be humbled, and those who humble themselves will be exalted."
Luke 14:7-11 NLT

In the parable above, Christ is telling us not to think too much of ourselves. When we think too much of ourselves, one of two things will happen. One: we will embarrass ourselves when someone who has accomplished more than we have shows up.

Alternatively, two: we will not be humble enough to serve others. In my opinion, the second is worse than the first. We must be in humble positions to serve others. This means that we must not think that we are better than we really are.

Because of the privilege and authority God has given me, I give each of you this warning: Don't think you are better than you really are. Be honest in your evaluation of yourselves, measuring yourselves by the faith God has given us. Romans 12:3 NLT

We must be able to show others the love of God. This is what he asks of us. We are to serve others. We are not to retaliate when things go wrong in our lives, instead we are to "give the other cheek." We cannot do this if we are filled with pride that will not allow us to serve others or God.

I have found myself in a peculiar season in my life boasting in how much I serve. I have heard myself and others list off all the things that they have done "in the name of Jesus." People say things like: "I sing in the choir, am president of XYZ organization, and head up the hospitality committee. I am serving the Lord with every part of me." If someone tells you this clearly as a way of boasting, then this is the only reward they will receive.

"Watch out! Don't do your good deeds publicly, to be admired by others, for you will lose the reward from your Father in heaven…. But when you give to someone in need, don't let your left hand know what your right hand is doing. Give your gifts in private, and your Father, who sees everything, will reward you.
Matthew 6:1-4 NLT

We have to be humble servants of God and through this we will receive our reward in heaven. I would much rather receive eternal rewards in heaven than physical rewards down here that will perish when I do.

The hip-hop artist, Lecrae, says in his song, *Rebel vs. Gravity*:

"Hey man I still believe everything I wrote on Rebel. You know what I mean?
Me bragging about where I been or what kinda mission trips I'm doing And who I'm discipling And so on and so forth in every song doesn't make me more holy. And me not talking about it doesn't make me less holy. It's all grace baby. I hope we can have graces with me, As the Lord has been gracious to us all"

I can identify. The song is a dialogue between the old Lecrae in his earlier albums to the newer more transformed Lecrae from his later albums. It is so easy for me to say "I did all of these things for God. Look at how great I am. Love me!" These thoughts and words do not give true service to God. They are services to myself. As I grow in Christ, I am learning to be less vocal and more giving. I am also learning how to care about what God says about me more than any person here on earth. Hearing that God thinks I'm great is worth more than any words anyone else could give me.

Jesus not only washed feet, but he died on a cross. Death on a cross at that time was the worst death that anyone could experience. It was shameful. Death on a cross meant that you committed the most horrendous crime, though we know the Christ never committed any sin. This is the ultimate act of selfless service.

We may never be able to measure up to this level of service, but that does not mean we do not try. In order to serve like Christ, we must be ready to receive no credit for the work we have done. We do this first because we accomplish nothing without the Lord; therefore we should give the credit to God. Secondly, if we are to live a life like Christ, it means we are to live without pride. Recognition for good work is, however, a good thing and we should honor those who labor among us (1 Thessalonians 5:12).

Pride was once an issue in my life, but God humbled me while I was in high school. I did well academically in high school and was used to winning things and being at the top of the list for almost everything. I entered the Youth of the Year contest with my church my junior year of high school. I lost, twice. For a person like me who never lost anything, that shows how great I was academically or in the dozens of extracurricular activities that I was a part of, this was a major hit on my ego. I was devastated the first time I lost. I did not care as much the second time. God showed me that my ego was in the way the second go around. I'm so glad that God taught me that lesson in high school because in college, and now in graduate school, I have lost many contests and have received lower grades than I thought I deserved. I have tried out for things and jobs that I did not receive. I now see that my life is not always about me, and in those situations, I look towards God to show which way I should be going instead.

Christ worked

In His defense Jesus said to them, My Father is always at His work to this very day, and I too am working.
John 15:17 NIV

In the above verse, Jesus was defending his action of healing on the Sabbath, a day when no work should ever occur. He was defending himself to the people that would eventually crucify him. The religious people at the time were always trying to trap him into breaking the law in order to kill him. Jesus did not break any law. He was perfect.

Christ was always on the move. He got a lot accomplished in his three years of ministry. There are many times when the bible talks about Christ being on a boat moving from one city to another. I am not saying that we should all move every three years, although God has called some of us to that exact thing. I am saying that we need to be dynamic in ministry. This means that we are not stagnant but rather constantly preaching the gospel, learning more about God and sharpening the weapons He has equipped us with.

I must admit I am not good at this. I keep myself busy, yet I am not always working. At point in my life, I joined the Connect Team at church (the greeting team), I was a youth leader, was a part of two lifegroups, in graduate school and had a part time job. Busy does not even describe that period of my life, but was I working for the Lord?

We must be careful not to fall into the trap that I so often fall into. We believe that because we are a part of five ministries, we are working. Yes, you are working hard but not working smart. God has showed me that I waste a lot of time. I literally waste hours a day not being productive. God has shown me that I must work smart and be effective in everything I do, even in my resting time. The Lord has called me to be excellent in everything. Yes, there are days that I fall short, but excellence is always the goal.

If the ministry is not fruitful and the people around us are not growing, we need to pray to see if this is the place God wants us to be. Maybe the ministry is not working because it is <u>not</u> supposed to be led by you, or because as my mother would say, it's a "good idea but not a God idea." We must consider these things when praying about where the Lord wants us. If the ministry is for you ask God to give you wisdom on how to be effective. God wants us to succeed.

Christ worked, but he was not busy. He took time to talk to children and heal people that merely touched Him in the street. I have to be more in tune with the Lord and learn not to be busy but rather work for the Lord. When I become so busy that I cannot take care of the people that pop-up in life that need my aid, my focus is on the wrong things.

God wants us to be led by the Holy Spirit, and not always by our schedules. I am not saying that you should throw away your schedule and never look at it again. I am saying that there is balance and you have to make room in your day to bless others. We cannot move so fast from place to place that we do not notice people that need God's encouragement along the way.

I know that there are times when I find myself wanting to quit everything in life. I know of many other people that have felt the same way. Then I am reminded that this is my purpose right now. I am a single person with not even a dog to take care of. My life should be geared toward doing the Lord's work outside of my home (1 Corinthians 7:34).

I realized that I still have to find the balance between being busy and working for the Lord. I believe that God has a place for me to work for Him and not be busy. God wants us to enjoy the lives that he gave us.

Christ sacrificed.

Whoever says he abides in Him ought to walk in the same way in which he walked. 1 John 2:6 ESV

The verse above says that if we abide in Christ, we should live the life he lived. To me this means that the Lord gave His life for us and we should do the same for others. My favorite New Testament verse is Mark 14:36:

"Abba, Father," he cried out, "everything is possible for you. Please take this cup of suffering away from me. Yet I want your will to be done, not mine." NLT

Jesus is the model for our time on earth. Right before he goes to the cross, Jesus asks the Lord to take this horrible death away from Him. But Jesus is so obedient that he dies on the cross anyway. It is my favorite verse because it shows that although He was sent directly from God, Jesus was also human. God asks us to do hard things on His behalf all of the time. Like Jesus, we must be willing to do the hard things no matter how our flesh feels about it. Jesus submitted His will to God's will and we should too.

Remembering Mark 14:36 helps me put my life in perspective. I used to complain when I have to pick up the youth that lives across town because of the high cost of gas. I used to complain when I have to stay up past my bedtime to get work done for church or school. God is so much bigger; he sacrificed so much more for me. How dare I complain about staying awake for a youth lock-in or typing a paper at 1:00 AM?

Sacrifice for me looks like waking up at the time I am supposed to and reading my bible instead of going back to sleep. It means giving my last $5.00 in the offering plate Sunday when I know I won't have money until the following Friday. The Lord calls us to sacrifice and it looks different for all people. Sacrifices are a form of worship. I have to remember this when I am in worship at my church and I am afraid to lift my hands or am afraid to sing loud. The Lord wants us to look "foolish" in the world's eyes for him (1 Peter 2:9). Change happen in the sacrifice.

As I am letting the Lord guide me into what sacrifices he wants from me, I know that it's not going be all fun and games. If that were the case, it would not be a sacrifice. I remember Mark 14:36 and how much Jesus loved us to sacrifice for us and I get over it. I get over it by realizing that it is only a short period of time that will lead to lasting changes in my life. I know when God asks me for something, I will get more from him.

I usually feel peace after I have given up something that I want for something that he has for me. I had the opportunity to go England with my graduate school for about a month that would cause me to miss a few events here in the United States. I had so much anxiety around the trip. I knew that God was asking me not to go and to stay here but I could not understand why God would ask me to give up an opportunity like this. The first event I would have missed was youth camp with the youth at my church. I eventually went to youth camp and it was one of the best experiences of my life. I was introduced to a new way to minister to youth. I met a great group of youth that I will never forget and I pray that I will be able to pour into their lives after that one week. The second event I would have possibly missed was the national convention of my home church. I am so glad that I went. I was able to reconnect with people from my church and was refreshed with new and old friendships. When I gave up my selfish desire, the Lord gave me so much more. There will be more opportunities to go to England, but not many opportunities to pour into the lives of the youth or the church.

Let us think of the sacrifices of Jesus in another way. Jesus, God's only son, came down from heaven to die for all of our sin, hurt, and shame. Jesus, who was perfect in all he did, gave us filthy, unworthy people undeserved love and a second chance to make it right with God. In order to make it right with God, we must believe in Jesus and that he came here to save us.

...because, if you confess with your mouth that Jesus is Lord and believe in your heart that God raised him from the dead, you will be saved Romans 10:9ESV

Praise God that he loved us enough to sacrifice his life, so that we might be saved!

Christ spent precious time with God, Our Father.

And when it was day, he departed and went into a desolate place. And the people sought him and came to him, and would have kept him from leaving them,
Luke 4:42 ESV

But Jesus Himself would often slip away to the wilderness and pray. Luke 5:16 NASB

And it came to pass in those days, that he went out into a mountain to pray, and continued all night in prayer to God. Luke 6:12 KJV

The "He" mentioned in the three scriptures above are all Jesus. The Lord went alone to talk to God. This was where he got strength and direction to deal with us. Jesus went off to pray by himself. He talked to God without others around. He took time out to show us and God how important this time was. All direction and healing comes from God. If I need direction and peace I run to God. If I need love and joy, I run to God. I believe this is what Jesus did also.

People that have time with God on a daily basis are so different from those of us that do not. I can tell when someone spends time with God daily and listens to Him. They are usually calm people that do not react to every wrong thing that happens in their lives. I usually say, "He/she really knows Jesus," after a conversation with them. These people have the spirit of the Jesus in them. When you live that closely with the Spirit it is hard for you to act in fleshly ways. The biggest distinction of people that spend time with God everyday is that they are loving and gentle.

There are examples in the Bible of what happens when someone spends time with God. In Exodus 34:29-35, Moses's face shone after he spent time with God on the mountain. In Acts 4:13, the high priest were astonished that Peter and John were normal, but they could not deny that Peter and John spent time with Jesus.

Like Moses, Peter, and John, there are noticeable differences in my life when I spend time with God. I operate either out of His son or out of my flesh. As a fleshly mess, I have the tendency to be mean and have absolutely no compassion for others. This comes out when I have not read the Bible in a few days, sat down and talked to God, or worshiped him. The Lord is the one who moves me from my fleshy desires and defaults of being rude to being like him. I HAVE to connect with God to stop my flesh from taking over in every aspect of my life. In my time with God, my spirit grows and my flesh dies.

The Lord wants us to know him. He wants us to come close to him and to receive our spiritual daily bread. The word tells us that he gives us enough for the day and that today's troubles are enough for today. This is the way we are to live and come back to him each day for him to take off the burdens and to give us enough grace for the day. I spend time with God to get my daily bread and to understand who God is. I want to see him in a new way. Many times, I read Psalm 119:33-40 where the writer asks God to show him more of the commandments that God has put in place. The Psalmist asks God:

Teach me your decrees, O LORD; I will keep them to the end. Give me understanding and I will obey your instructions; I will put them into practice with all my heart.
Psalm 119:33-34 NLT

In order to learn the decrees of God, I know that I must spend time with him and with his word. There is no other way to learn.

Spending time with God is such an integral part of our walk with God. My mother has been late for work or other events because she hadn't finished her devotional time. She knows the importance of spending time with Jesus. I used to question her about this, but now I understand. We operate at our optimal level when we take time to talk to Jesus. I must admit I do not have this down packed but I work toward this everyday.

We must spend time with God, Jesus, and the Holy Spirit. This time looks different for different people. It could mean singing for an hour or it could mean reading the word for 30 minutes. I heard someone say that for a time in their life, they spent time with Jesus while looking at galaxy videos on YouTube. During that time, they thanked God for His brilliance and saw how small they were in comparison to God and what he created. Whatever way we spend time with God, we must do it in a way that is from our hearts.

In my quiet time, I have written songs and gained wisdom on how to communicate with others. The most important thing for me is that I spend time with him to show him how much he means to me. I receive vision for my life and see how the pieces of my life will fall into place as I continue on the path he has for me.

Whatever we do in life, we should spend time with God and learn his voice. Jesus Christ did it, so we should too. These are the two most important things that you can do as you grow your walk with the Lord. Spending time with Jesus has saved me embarrassment numerous times. Once there was a guy at church that threw mixed signals, which caused me to think I liked him. Consequently, I told the Lord and all of my friends that I was going to confront him about it. God told me not to. I was so glad that I spent time with God not only to tell him what I was going to do but to ask Him what I should actually do. After I saw the gentleman again, I realized that I did not like him. Actually, he was not my type at all. Spending time with God saved me embarrassment and beginning a relationship that I did not even want.

Go ye therefore

I was having a conversation one day attempting to convince one of my friends NOT to get a doctoral degree. His response was "Why not? Knowledge is power." I immediately responded "No it's not." At the time, I was thinking about the doctoral program I am currently in and how I will have a degree. If I end up not getting a job in sociology, I will have all of this knowledge that might not be of much benefit to me in say a job teaching math at a high school. I also thought about my friend in pharmacy school that hates it. He knows that he will not be a pharmacist after the four years of school are done. In my opinion, pharmacy knowledge does not do much good outside of the medical field.

I reflected later about the conversation and how

quickly I said knowledge is not power. I decided that knowledge is power but actions backed by knowledge are even more powerful. We so often have information and do nothing with it. I am a doer, so my view of this is a little skewed. I think about the many lessons my parents taught me and I did not take heed. I learned right from wrong, but chose not to use the information given to me. Think about how many convicting sermons you have heard. After you hear them, you go back living your life the way you always have. Knowledge is power, but more powerful when action occurs.

Action backed by sound knowledge is what will change the world. Even after we have both knowledge and action, if there is no love, we have done nothing.

If I could speak all the languages of earth and of angels, but didn't love others, I would only be a noisy gong or a clanging cymbal. If I had the gift of prophecy, and if I understood all of God's secret plans and possessed all knowledge, and if I had such faith that I could move mountains, but didn't love others, I would be nothing. If I gave everything I have to the poor and even sacrificed my body, I could boast about it; but if I didn't love others, I would have gained nothing. 1 Corinthians 13:1-3 NLT

Jesus tells us to:

Go ye therefore, and teach all nations, baptizing them in the name of the Father, and of the Son, and of the Holy Ghost: Matthew 28:19 KJV

The first word in the verse is a verb; "Go." The Lord has called me to go to places where I am sometimes uncomfortable. The second verb in the verse is "teach." In order to teach someone a subject or topic, we must first know it and learn it. God is showing me this now. I must pray daily to Him. I must read the Bible. As the Lord teaches me, I have things to teach others. The last verb in the verse is "baptizing." God calls each of us to go, teach, and baptize people in his name. This verse isn't only a command for preachers or missionaries, but is a command for all of us. Matthew 9:35 tells us about Jesus going throughout the land and sharing the good news of the kingdom. Jesus did everything he tells us to do.

I now know that I had a flawed thinking of what Christ did. I thought because Christ preached and spread the truth that I could not possibly do the same. Only people with a special calling, a special vision from God, can go and teach in the villages and towns. I now know that I am supposed to live like Christ, I am to go to people and tell them about God. I am to tell others the truth.

I am ready to be a worker to harvest the field that God has prepared specifically for me. I cannot wait for God to continue to show me his plan for the ministry that I am to lead, start, or work with. God has a plan and a purpose for every person on earth and a major part of that purpose is to lead others to him. I know that I am gaining skills at this stage of life that I will use later on.

What does looking like Christ look like for you?

There is a song by Ronald Julian called *WWJD.* In the song he says, "You're the hands and feet of Christ, if you want to know what he looks like, he looks like you,

Jesus looks like you."

Jesus said that the greatest two commandments were to love God and love our neighbor as ourselves (Mark 12:29-31). He knew if we loved our neighbors as ourselves we would not treat them with disrespect, curse them out, look at them funny, lust after their husband/wife, etc. I challenge you each day to treat at least one person that you do not like or have a hard time dealing with like you would treat yourself in the same situation. Have a little compassion and give a little mercy. It will go a long way. We are to put off who we once were and put on who God is in his righteousness and holiness.

I saw this change in my own life as I have grown in the Lord. I used to have anger problems. I would cuss someone either in my brain or in real life for saying one wrong thing to me. I remember going off on a boyfriend and throwing an ICEE at him. Please do not judge me, it was a truth of my life. I can no longer imagine myself throwing a drink at anyone out of anger. It actually surprised me that I used to do things like that.

To put off your old self, which belongs to your former manner of life and is corrupt through deceitful desires, and to be renewed in the spirit of your minds, and to put on the new self, created after the likeness of God in true righteousness and holiness. Ephesians 4:22-24 ESV

One day while I was praying, God spoke this verse to me in my quiet time. He told me "they hated me first." In my quest to look more and more like Christ I might be hated by others. Ridicule, gossip, and the lack of support come with truly following Jesus.

Once in college I had a friend, who was raised going to church her entire life. For some reason she did not understand where I came from on a lot issues. I do not remember any specific occasion, but I knew that I always felt ostracized at the end of each of our conversations. I always felt like I was wrong for believing what I believed. I never stopped being myself around her. I knew God's word is true. I knew that I could not change my wording to make others more comfortable.

"If the world hates you, remember that it hated me first. John 15:18 NLT

Be true to Christ. Not to yourself.

So now what?

In this chapter, I introduced a lot of roles Christ had and still has today for us. As Christians, we are on a journey to be more like Christ. There is at least one of those roles that Christ filled that we can work on in our own lives. What do you need to work on? If you cannot pinpoint at least one area, ask God to tell you. Lord what in me can be transformed to look more like Christ? Reveal these things to me and remind me daily to implement these things into my life. He is faithful to answer you.

For some of us, we may need to be honest with ourselves and own up to the fact that we are not practicing Christians. For those of us who are practicing, what area can we improve in? Do you need to love others better? Do you need to spend more time with God? For each section above there are two or three questions that you can critically ask yourself and God to grow in that area.

Christ Loves

Christ loves us unconditionally, no matter what we do. What causes me not to love others fully? How can I remove that item, emotion, or person from my life? Am I looking at people around me the way God does?

Christ Discipled

Christ took time in his ministry to show others the truth and the way to live. Am I being discipled? Am I discilping others? Who around me can disciple me or can I disciple? What in my life do I have to get rid of to make time to disciple others fully?

Christ Served Others

Christ served with little to no recognition until His death. Am I serving at all? Are there needs in my church or community that I can fill? Am I serving in order to get recognition for the service that I am doing?

Christ Worked

Christ worked to help build the Kingdom of God. Am I currently doing anything to help build the Kingdom of God? Are there ways to incorporate working for God in the things that I am already doing?

Christ Sacrificed

Christ paid the ultimate sacrifice when he died on the cross for our sins. Am I giving my life for God or for others? What sacrifices in my life are God asking of me that I am not giving? Are there areas of over-indulgences that I should cut back on to get closer to God?

Christ Spent Time with God

Christ went away and spent time with God by himself. Am I spending time with God daily to see what he has for me? Can I add more time at the beginning of my day in order for this to happen?

Christ Spread the Truth

Christ shared who he was with the world. Am I sharing the Gospel with others? Are there ways I can spread the word of God in my community without changing my daily activities? How can I add this to my life?

2 failing others-life of an example

In the same way, let your light shine before others, so that they may see your good works and give glory to your Father who is in heaven. Matthew 5:16 ESV

To all my past and present friends, coworkers, family members, and all others I have had some form of close contact with, I am sorry. I am publicly apologizing to you for not looking like Christ at all times. My temporary lack of Godly standards has caused others to stumble and I will give an account to God for this one day. Second, I want to say that I believe in a God that redeems and does not look at our past, but at our present and future. Therefore, I pray that you look not at my past actions, but what I am today and forevermore.

Everything we do in life is premeditated whether it is underneath or in the forefront of our minds. Whether we want to admit what the cause is or not, there is a cause. I do not like confrontation. I know that I have a strong personality, which makes people believe I have strong opinions. I learned that my tone and speech pattern was a turn off for many people. So instead of stating how I feel at the expense of making others mad, I learned to be silent. This new pattern of life became an over correction, instead of learning how to use my tone and words to express myself in a way that would not turn others off.

After the Lord saves you, He gradually reveals areas in your life that need to be changed. My life B.C. (before Christ) was one in which I did not care what I sounded like. I could care less who I hurt when I spoke. The only thing that mattered was that you heard my opinion. Because I felt so strongly about this, I did not care if you liked me afterwards or not. Needless to say, I made a lot of enemies because of this. People thought I was rude and cold - they were right.

One of the most vivid examples of my cold and heartless life occurred when I was in high school. I was in the band and there was always some type of drama, like most other high school settings. I remember distinctly standing near the center of the room and a classmate asking me if I liked one of the other girls in the band. I said, "No, I don't like her at all." Unfortunately, she was standing right behind me as this whole interaction was occurring. After I realized that she was standing behind me, I said, "I don't care. I still don't like her." It's okay not to like every individual in the world, but that interaction was totally inappropriate and did not glorify God. That was not one of my proudest moments in life.

A. C. (after Christ), I did not want to be rude and cold. That is not the love of Christ. So I did everything in my power to combat that. I feared seeing people from my past because I had no idea what I had done or said to them. It was especially scary if I was involved romantically with them in anyway. I did not know which

Jasmine they saw. This was not a good time in my life because I knew that I was changed, but other people in my life did not.

I wanted so badly for everyone to see the new me, the redeemed me, the loving, kind me. So in social interactions A.C., whether private or large social gatherings, I would oftentimes stay silent instead of spreading truth into the situation. It had gotten so bad that I would blame the silence on the Holy Spirit. I would say that the Lord did not want me to say anything in that situation. How crazy is that? That may have been true in some situations, but I know the Lord wants us to speak his truth and bring people out of the dark.

The over-correction had gotten so bad that it bled into my time with God. Normally, I would listen to music, sing, and write during my quiet time. I love to sing! Singing and music is how I connect to God, and it is something that He has called me to do. But I wouldn't sing for Him. I would just sit and literally not be able to open my mouth even when God told me to. In order to break the silence, I had to write a chorus to a song, one that would make me open my mouth and sing praises to God.

> "I won't be silent
> I won't be silent
> I can't be quiet
> You've been too good"

I have learned that I need to speak when the Lord wants me to. I had to break the silence in my mind and open my mouth. After further thought, I realized that some of the silence stemmed from insecurity.

Insecurities built up from years of looking crazy when I talked to others about God. Sometimes I just want to look "normal." I did not want to be the crazy person always talking about Jesus. I learned that I cannot let my insecurities take the place of what God has placed in me.

I have gotten visions and drawn pictures of myself opening my mouth and love, peace, and joy flowing out. I have had to break my barrier of silence in order to accomplish this step in my life to the fullest. I know that God wants me to live a full life that centers on me sharing his love, peace, and joy with others.

Failure in ministry

One of my many passions (if you haven't picked this up yet) is youth ministry. Although it is my passion, it is by far one of the scariest things in my life at this point. Do you know how it feels for a parent to tell you that his or her children look up to you? That's scary! Knowing that someone younger than you is watching your interactions and will mimic the actions and words that you use is terrifying. Although it is okay to make mistakes, the perception is that you cannot make mistakes. Being someone that people can look up to adds great pressure.

I have failed the youth time after time. Time after time. Time after time. When I am not prepared spiritually and mentally the youth suffer. When I do not take the time to plan a good game for them to play on Wednesday nights, I have failed them.

When I am not spiritually prepared it is even worse.

When I am not having consistent and meaningful time with the Lord, I have nothing to offer the youth. There have been times when they have asked me a serious question and instead of running to Holy Spirit I would run to a default answer that sounds halfway religious. Looking back now, I see that honestly would actually have been the best answer. Telling a 17-year-old girl, " I do not know the answer. I will get back to you," or, "Let's ask God together," is way better than saying, "Because the Lord won't put more on you than you can bear," or some other cliché I do not know I believe myself.

Not only have I failed the youth, but I have failed others that I was supposed to minister to. I heard a preacher once share the encounter with a man that He witnessed to. The man asked the preacher "If you all believe what you say you believe, why do you keep it to yourself? This is selfish." The "you all" in the above quote is us, followers of Christ, and the "it" is the Gospel of Jesus Christ. After the preacher shared, I was amazed. Either I am selfish, or I want other people to go to hell. Neither explanation is good, yet they are the only two explanations for not sharing the Gospel. I know that it is not that I want others to go to hell, so I must be selfish. The preacher was right; we are selfish. I am selfish. I need to share the Gospel with all people always, not just on Sundays after the pastor convicts us or when we are on a one-week mission to trip to some foreign land. We must share every day. If we believe what the word says is true, it is our joy to share the gift of Jesus Christ with others.

The Holy Spirit encourages me to talk to people all of the time, but sometimes I literally feel like I cannot open my mouth. I am a talkative person who never really has a problem talking. When the Lord says, "Tell them how good I am," or "Tell them about me," I cannot do it. Sometimes, the fear of humans is too much for me to bear on my own. I know this is wrong and I know that I need help through this but it is real. I know that I cannot be afraid of looking "crazy." I know that I must show others the love of God through my words.

I tell myself, when my ministry becomes my full time job, I will not care. Only the Lord knows if this is my path. Ministry may never be my full time job. As my friend would say I do believe "my life is my ministry"; my actions speak more than my words.

We can't wait until tomorrow to tell people about Jesus. We have to start now. Tell them now how good it is to feel the peace that He gives us. Tell them about the unexplainable joy. Tell them that there is always hope for tomorrow in Jesus. Tell them about how good God is. Tell them how loving Jesus is. Tell them how patient the Holy Spirit is. When we do this, lives are changed and transformed for the better. People are introduced to Jesus! Tell them as one of my favorite artists, Mali Music, says in a song, "You're not only the best thing that happened to me, but you're simply the best thing that ever happened."

Failure in ministry for me comes from many different sources. I fail when I am disobedient to the Holy Spirit. Two times in my life God has used others when he actually called me. Once on a mission trip and another time at church. Before I went on a mission trip to the Dominican Republic, the Lord gave me visions of who to pray for and how they would get healed. While on the trip, I saw the exact man I was supposed to pray for. It was awesome! I did not go pray for him though. I was excessively scared. A few moments later, I saw two young men that were on the trip with me praying for the man, and it was then I went over. The Lord showed me this man weeks before but I did not have enough courage to pray.

I learned a couple of things from this moment in my life. The first is that God will heal whom he wants to heal whether we obey him or not. The second is that God wants obedience from us in the moment. If I could do it all over again I would run over to that hurting man and pray from him. There would be no hesitation and no doubt in me.

At church one Sunday, a young woman had a word from the Lord, but it was in the form of tongues. I knew that I had the interpretation for those tongues, but someone went up before so I thought that I was wrong and I did not go up. But after they were done "interpreting" the tongue I felt that it was not correct. I still did not go up, someone else had the correct interpretation, and of course it matched the words the Lord gave me.

I know that God completes his tasks with or without me but I would much rather be used by God than sit on the sidelines watching others do his work. Once you accept Jesus into your heart, the fun begins. You then go on adventures with him to cleanse yourself and show others his love. I used to only want Jesus to cleanse me and fix my problems. I now see that God has a purpose for my life. I know this and I do not want Him to give my assignment to someone else.

Failure in relationships

I like people. I like having people around and if I truly love you as a person, I care about what you think of me. It is so hard for me to say, "No," to certain groups of people. I just want everyone to like me. I took a strengths test and one of the my strengths is "Woo." A person with "woo" characteristics "love the challenge of meeting new people and winning them over. They derive satisfaction from breaking the ice and making a connection with another person" (Rath,169). This is absolutely a part of my personality. As you can imagine, this is a lot of pressure at times. But inherently, people are different which means that being funny might be important to one person, and being calm may be important to another. As a result, I was endlessly changing to make others happy, happy enough to like me.

This strength, when not used correctly, can cause personal issues. It did that for me, especially during my undergraduate education. It seemed like people did not see me as the person I thought I was. On many occasions, people would tell me who they thought I was and their perceptions did not always match with what I thought of myself. I realized that I showed people a version of me that I thought they would like, not my genuine self. Constantly changing, I failed to show who Christ was in me; the true and real Jasmine.

I failed a lot in romantic relationships. Too many times I told a boy I'm a Christian, just to do unholy things with him, like lie to him, or fornicate. Yes there is grace. Yes, we fall sometimes, but that is not an excuse. I knew the consequences of sin. My unbelieving boyfriend on the other hand did not, nor would He find out by being in a relationship with me. I know now that I was not mature enough to be in a romantic relationship of any kind; it was not the right choice for a 17-year-old girl who did not know how to control her emotions.

Lastly, I have failed in the relationships that I have with those younger than me. I have a few "little bothers" and a few "little sisters" (they are not related to me by blood) in my life that I try to show how to live a Christian life. It's hard though as I navigate the world through my new spiritual eyes. The Lord has shown me that failing is a part of life and that it is okay to do so. I can share this with my little brothers and sisters and show them how to handle failure with more grace than me. I want to teach them to learn from my mistakes and not go down a path that I have already gone down. I heard one Sunday at my home church, "learn from the example, don't be the example."

Failure in school

High school came easy. Every class that did not come easy, I took my 'B' and kept moving. When I graduated college, I looked at my mom and whispered, "I could have worked harder. I could have had a higher GPA." I did not ever put my best foot forward when it came to school. Because I was not failing any classes, no teacher was concerned. Work ethic, especially if I thought the class was pointless, was what I was missing. These problems did not stop when I went to graduate school.

I like to think that I work with excellence in everything that I do, but this is not the case. I often drop the ball on many projects (mostly academic) that I have absolutely no passion for. As I finish a course or write a paper, I often wonder how this is going to help people suffering from social injustices or how this is going help the Kingdom of God grow.

Some days I want to quit. Graduate school is hard and uneventful. But the Lord reminds me that I am here for a purpose. I have realized that not every moment of my life will be bells and whistles as the world wants me to believe. Some of life is hard and uneventful and you just have to do it to get to where God wants you to be.

We as followers of Christ must remember to serve God in everything we do. For me that looks like praying for my officemate to get through a rough semester or encouraging other students to do better in classes.

My failure became evident two times in my life in the form of two "wake-up calls." During the first, a classmate asked me with a straight face, if I was going to quit the program. I saw that I was not putting my best foot forward in school. If I were putting my best foot forward, she would not have any reason to ask me this question. I needed to work on excellence in how I present myself to others and how I see school as a whole. I knew at that moment that I was not doing either one of those things. No, graduate school is not fun, but I know that it is necessary for whatever God has planned next for me. Grad school is a part of my path and I am not going to quit. God wants me here. I must start working with excellence.

A conversation I had with my mother was the second "wake-up call". While complaining about the plight of graduate school, she reminded me that God would never tell me the purpose of this part of my life until I stopped complaining about it. I knew then that I must stop being angry that I cannot see or feel the immediate benefits of graduate school and realize that there is a plan for every step we take. God has a purpose and every class and every paper, can be used to the glory of God if I allow it to be.

I will no longer fail at school. I will no longer talk about school as if it is the worst part of my life. I see now that I must be light in a dark place. I am not the only person in graduate school that is not totally satisfied. I have the Lord. I know that there is light at the end of the tunnel. Not all people know this. I must learn to act and speak as if I know this truth.

Failure to my family

I pray often for the salvation of my family members. Now it is time for me to lead by example. No longer will I hide my beliefs and laugh at jokes that I should not laugh at. There were many times that I was misunderstood. I'm no longer apologizing. I love talking to and being around other people who are also trying to look like Christ.

God is real. Christ is real. The Holy Spirit is real. If you look at the people God used in the Bible, the only one that did not screw up was Jesus. That is why he is the model. We are all examples to the world, but our purpose is to point them to Christ. We do not have to live this life on our own. The Holy Spirit is with us to guide us to God.

One of my best friends tells me, "My life is a ministry." I now know what that means. Every day, I am to show redemption and love through my character, even to those who are closest to me. From now on I pledge to make my life my ministry. No, I will not be perfect, but I will daily die to myself and be a servant of others. This is the way Jesus lived and the way we should all live.

Failure to myself

Failures in all of the above areas led to me believe that I was failing myself. I had guilt from past relationships. I kept thinking, "How many of my ex-boyfriends could I have pointed to the Lord. How many friends? How many roommates?" My only job was to live a life that resembles Christ and share my beliefs. I did not even do that fully. I could not even tell people why I lived the life I live.

I had so much shame from the gunk in my heart. My conceitedness, literal hate for people, and the grudges I held were taking over. There was so much inside of me that needed releasing in order for God to use me.

I used to have internal dialogue when I went around certain people. I had to pump myself up not to fall into the temptation I knew I was walking straight into. Soon internal conflicts about the life I wanted to live and the one I was actually living arose. I did not know how to overcome them. I kept living a sinful life, but I was having convicting thoughts. This reminds me of the lyrics of a song by Jonathan McReynolds that says: "And I don't wanna keep going to church/Singing all about how much You're worth/And then continue doing my dirt/Living as if I didn't care if You're hurt." That was my life. I have gone to church my whole life, so I was surrounded by people that loved Jesus, and I did too, but I still lived as if God did not exist.

Our bodies are wired to express pain physically if we hold on to our emotions long enough. Sometimes the spiritual and internal issues that we have manifest themselves as physical or psychological ones and that was happening with me. The days that I was living a double life, I would stay awake at night and found no rest. During that time, I bit down so hard on my teeth that my jaw would hurt and I had to get a special mouth guard made to sleep with. It was bad for quite some time. I could not sleep for about two years and my jaws would continually hurt.

When you have psychological aliments like headaches, stomachaches, depression, and anxiety, ask the Lord about the source of the issue. There is no sickness that He cannot handle. The cross heals us not only spiritually, but also mentally and physically as well.

But he was pierced for our transgressions; He was crushed for our iniquities; upon him was the chastisement that brought us peace, and with his wounds we are healed.
Isaiah 53:5 ESV

One of my biggest issues was telling myself that I was worthy of what God has for me. If I looked at my life for everything that it was and saw everything that I lacked, and then take a look at what the Lord was still giving me. It's crazy. The Lord still gives. He still loves. He still cares.

No longer am I bound by my guilt and my shame. I no longer live a life where past experiences scare me or bring up bad memories. I am truly free from all my past. The spirit of the Lord lives inside of me. The word of God confirms this:

Now the Lord is the Spirit, and where the Spirit of the Lord is, there is freedom.
2 Corinthians 3:17 ESV

I participated in a prayer ministry called Sozo, which means saved, healed, or delivered in the Greek. During this process, you sit down with a trained session leader and they guide you with the help of God, Jesus, and the Holy Spirit to heal areas that are deep and that you might not have even known were broken. As humans, we have spiritual doors in our lives that we can let open. Some are good like the door to forgiveness, and some are bad like the door to bitterness. In the process, I closed many doors that I let open by curiosity and sin. I forgave people I did not even know I was mad at. For example, we closed the door I opened to sexual sin, and I forgave the first person that ever touched me that way. I did not even know I had negative feelings toward him. I honestly had not thought about him in years. We have to be careful to what we open doors to in our lives.

I live a transparent life now, but I am committing to be more transparent with my failures and my heartaches and struggles with life. I realized that there is no sense or reason to keep my struggles to myself. Testimonies set people free.

Once my friend was sharing how hard it was for her to spend time with God, and everyone in the room was feeling the same way. We all shared our issues with each other and discussed how we can help each other out in this area. Because she spoke up, we all gained freedom in this area.

After God transformed and changed my life, some things had to change. Although the Lord made me a fighter, I was fighting the wrong things. I was fighting on his behalf, but was not using the correct language or was still having a horrible attitude. God did not want me to fight that way anymore, especially on behalf of him. He told me that I was even fighting him at times. This is not what God created me to do. He wants me to stand firm, not fight. At the point in my life where the Lord revealed this, I was still in a guilt stage. I took every correction from God not as correction but as criticism, and instead of fixing the correction I sometimes got worse or did nothing because I did not want to deal with the issue at all. I now know that God is my corner and I am to love him with my whole heart and to take his love for me in the form of correction.

Put on all of God's armor so that you will be able to stand firm against all strategies of the devil.
Ephesians 6:11 NLT

Misconceptions

I realized that not only do I fail others, and myself but oftentimes I am misunderstood. Not that you have to understand me to love me, but when witnessing to others it can be challenging for them to understand the message of Christ if they cannot understand the messenger. I soon realized that people thought that since I was a Christian I must be perfect. Being a follower of Christ meant that I did not know what it meant to feel pain or be sad. It was like we magically are supernatural people that don't live on earth. This is not that case. I have to pay bills just like everyone else.

There is a song by Lecrae ft W.L.A.K. entitled "Misconception Pt. 2" that speaks on this topic. The chorus says: "We're flawless and we think we're better/ Its official got it all together/We don't want 'em getting the wrong impressions/ Cause that ain't real that's a misconception/Been a struggle only Jesus kept us/And we still fall, so it's hard to get up/We don't want 'em getting the wrong impressions/Cause this is real ain't no misconception"

His lyrics also say that it has "been a struggle, only Jesus kept us." This is the testimony of every person that decides to follow Christ. We have the same struggles as everyone else. But it seems as if my friends and family do not always get that. I have heard two extremes about the way I live my life. The first extreme is that my life is perfect and nothing bad has ever happened to me. The second extreme is that I am a hypocrite, which is so funny to me. We cannot measure our struggles against another person's struggles. If something is a big deal in my life, then it is a big deal regardless of how it measures up to others people's lives. I no longer judge others based on what they are going through. I no longer say "that's it?!" when people tell me their problems. I listen and attempt to send them toward God. Our struggles are different. We all have to go to Christ at different times in our lives and ask for his help.

At one point in my life, losing or breaking my cell phone would have been the worst thing to happen to me. I probably would have been sad and prayed forever about it. Now, although I love my cell phone, it is not an issue if I lose it. I now see this situation in another light. I know that it is just a cell phone. I realized that most material possessions end up in the trash at some point. They will rust, break, or get lost. This is not to say that I do not take care of the items I own, I know that they should be idols in my life. Idols are things that can take the place of God. There are plenty of potential idols in material possessions. I realized that what matters is the condition of my heart and soul, both of which will last forever.

For others, losing or breaking a cell phone is the end of the world. It is a major problem for them. In those situations, I choose to point people to Jesus. I attempt to show them that Jesus cares about every need we have. He cares about our cares and wants to help us.

The other extreme that I hear from others about my life is that I am a horrible person and that I am actually a hypocrite. I hate the word *hypocrite* because it is overused in my opinion. From my perspective, the people that use the word to describe others know that they should be living a different life but are not. We have all been hypocrites at some point. A true hypocrite is one that "acts in contradiction to his or her stated beliefs or feelings." There are so many times that I say I don't believe in breaking the law, but I speed. I am not perfect, no follower of Christ is. But we are all in the race and fight together to move toward Christ. We are only responsible for ourselves. God, Jesus, and the Holy Spirit are the only measuring sticks we are to live by and we find these standards in the Bible. When we get to the end of our lives, God will not ask us what did the pastor of our church do in his lifetime, but rather what did we do.

In a late night conversation with a dear friend from Waco, we were discussing struggles and I shared with her that everyone that is in the world is also in the church. Cheats, liars, fornicators, idolaters, homosexuals, and some of the most prideful people you will ever meet are in the church. The difference is that know the truth. Knowing the truth does not make life automatically easier. People that do not believe in God can have knowledge of the truth. It actually makes certain aspects harder, without the power of God to overcome. After you begin to believe that God sent his son to die for you and confess with your mouth that this is true, Satan gets busier. Satan does not say, "Oh that's fine; God's got him/her," but rather, "I'm going to make them doubt; I'm going to attempt to deceive them more." You have to be prepared for what the devil brings. The church is not a place filled with people that have it all together. Rather, it is filled with people that are broken and know that they need the Lord to heal them. Life gets better because we have the power to overcome.

Through every misconception, I want one thing to known by all people. I want them to know that Christ loves them and can be their savior. No matter what else people see from others and me in the church, we must be honest with others and ourselves and show the world that God is bigger than anything else we are giving off to the world.

Leading by example

So whether you eat or drink, or whatever you do, do it all for the glory of God.
1 Corinthians 10:31 NLT

The Lord has called us all to be leaders. We can be leaders in our communities, families, and jobs. Wherever planted, the Lord wants us to be a leader there. I realized that people look at the life I live and often use me as an example. Because of this, I realized that I must lead by example and that failure in certain areas is no longer an option for the world that I live in.

I used to be a quitter. I rarely finished what I started. I quit the band and dancing in high school, soccer team in middle school, and I have quit the piano twice. I bought a guitar and know (maybe) three cords. I have not painted in years. I've joined about two or three gyms and workout classes. I can go on and on about the amount of money either my parents or I have wasted on me being too zealous and not committing.

Now I see that in all of these failures, there was growth. I learned something about myself in each stage. This is not an excuse to quit, but rather a truth that I have learned. I will continue to fall in different areas of my life, but God is always there. He shows me where I went wrong and how to change. I am not to make the same mistakes in 2 years, or 2 months, or even 2 weeks.

God has called me to be a leader and show others that he is faithful to the end. He shows me that there is no reason to quit and that he is with me in every new hobby that I want to pick up.

The most important thing I learned about failures so far is that not all failures are failures to God. Not getting a promotion, not making the soccer team, or a bankrupt business might be a part of his plan for you. Trust him in all things because he works all thing together for the good of us.

What now?

You just read all of the failures in my life that I have had on my own strength and how I have or plan to overcome them with the help of God. There is room to fail. Some "failures" are even from God. But those are only failures to the world's eyes. They are not failures to God.

Are there times in your life where the world has said that you failed but you clearly see God's hand?

Ask God to remind you of these times and show you how he provides in every situation.

Sometimes there are places of failure that we do not even know of until we ask God.

Ask God if there are places where you can improve or things you may not have known you need help in.

What have you failed by using your own strength?

Where was God in this situation?

What can you do different to improve in these areas?

Are there areas where you continually fail to show others Christ?

In addition to my failures without Jesus, I saw places for improvement in my life. The main one being making my life a ministry for others to see.

Do you view your life as ministry for others to see the true and living God?

God is faithful to help us improve in every area of our lives if we ask him.

jasmine wise

3 protection for greatness-guidance

Be strong, and let your heart take courage, all you who wait for the Lord! Psalm 31:24 ESV

God's plan is better, have faith.

If then you have been raised with Christ, seek the things that are above, where Christ is, seated at the right hand of God. Colossians 3:1 ESV

Fitting In

"This above all; to thine own self be true."
William Shakespeare

For we are his workmanship, created in Christ Jesus for good works, which God prepared beforehand, that we should walk in them. Ephesians 2:10 ESV

In graduate school, two individuals in ministry, which I did not know told me I would never fit in, so I should stop trying. I know that they were not trying to be mean, but rather give me a word from the Lord that I should not be trying to be like the world but live like Jesus instead.

As I look back, I realize that this theme has come up in my life many times. A friend of mine has called me weird since I met him in 2006. I never took offense. First, because I knew he was not trying to be hurtful. Secondly, because I did not care. My normal response was to laugh and move on. Apparently, I really am weird. Later on in life, one of my closet friends in undergrad told me that I was always doing my own thing. A cousin told me I was eclectic once. Apparently, other people always felt this way about me, I just did not know. The strangest thing for me is that I'm just living. I do not mean to be weird or to stand out.

When I reflect on high school and undergrad I realized that I was often out of place. I love to dance! Consequently, I went to parties and clubs, but I never looked right. I would attempt to keep up with my friends, but I never felt comfortable. I never made sense. I remember being stared at once in a club. I took offense; I dressed like everyone else and danced like everyone else. Those who were frequent there knew I was not supposed to be there. I now believe that others see things that we sometimes cannot.

I experienced similar situations with edifying and educational things. If I wait on my friends to join me in something I would never have the life or experience the world the way I want to. People get surprised when I go places by myself. They do not realize my choices are either to go by myself or to sit at home and watch television with my friends. (I love them don't get me wrong.) I would much rather be at a Harlem Globetrotter game, hear a lecture on poverty in America, or listen to the first black woman graduate of Baylor University.

I do not even always fit in at church either. I remember vividly being at choir rehearsal one day and the song was not easy for us to learn for some reason. I looked at everyone and said, "Let's just pray about it." I never felt as disconnected from a group as I did at that moment. I was confused that they were confused about my statement.

I realized now that the Lord made me this way because there are days that I must stand alone. I must speak the Truth no matter the cost. I have had practice being alone and not fitting in. It is a blessing rather than the curse that I first believed it was.

Do not be conformed to this world, but be transformed by the renewal of your mind, that by testing you may discern what is the will of God, what is good and acceptable and perfect. Romans 12:2 ESV

People that follow Christ always stand out. As I look back on people that I admire, they stand firm on the Lord. I look at them and say, "I can tell that he/she really knows Christ, they always make their own path." I see that they do not always fit in places.

There are times that all Christians must stand alone, but that is what we are called to do: To be set apart and be used by the Lord. Even in Christian communities I sometimes have to stand on what the Lord wants us to do no matter who agrees or disagrees with me. We must stand and do as he pleases. I want to thank God for this revelation. Someone has to be a trailblazer and a path maker. If not, there would never be any changes in the world.

Boys, Boys, Boys

You shall have no other gods before me.
Exodus 20:3 NIV

Attention from men was my idol.

Getting attention was easy in high school. For some reason when I went to college and broke up with my high school boyfriend something happened, no one seemed to give me the attention I grew accustomed to. I see now it was the Lord's protection over my life. I asked God one day why the guys I knew were interested in me were not talking to me. He told me he was protecting me. I always wondered from what but soon realized and saw all of the problems my friends were having with men. I saw the heartache and stress that came from being with men that God never intended us to be with.

This need for attention was fueled by my insecurities. I was so insecure that I either only flirted with the guys I already knew liked me or not intended to like back. I had sex with the ones I liked the most, and plenty of it. I prided myself in not having sex with more than one boy at a time or only after knowing him for years. I was so stupid. Yes, I gained pleasure out of the situation. Yes, I was using them for physical gain just like they were using me, but it was still wrong. Every time, I gave a piece of what was for my husband to someone who did not deserve it.

Because I was living this life someone once told me, "When you actually fall for a boy you are going to fall hard." and that is exactly what happened. I fell hard, so hard that I gave up my dignity toward the end of the relationship. I became a person that I did not even respect in this situation. I have since apologized and moved on with my life.

I made excuses for myself time after time. I said I was like King David in that I had a weakness for the opposite sex. I said if "David could be used by God then I can too!" These were lies, lies, and more lies. One of my friends happily reminded me that David "paid for those sins." I even tried to make a deal with God, that I should be given a pass once a year and it only be with the same person. I was literally out of my mind when I asked this, but God's patience and grace is real!

I am not one to blame the Lord for my sin. I do not sin accidentally; I know exactly what I am doing when I sin. I also know what the Bible says about temptation and sexual desires.

Run from sexual sin! No other sin so clearly affect the body as this one does. For sexual immorality is a sin against your own body. 1 Corinthians 6:18 NLT

Most other versions of the verse above say to "Flee from sexual immorality." I did not start fleeing until recently. The Lord has tried to save me at least twice that I could remember. In one situation, I did not take heed to the warnings. Afterwards, I counted and God gave me four chances to get out of the situation but I decided to stay where I was and sin. In the second situation, I took heed and left. Granted, I should have not put myself in the situation in the first place.

Temptation comes from our own desires, which entice us and drag us away. These desires give birth to sinful

actions. And when sin is allowed to grow, it gives birth to death.
James 1:14-15 NLT

I do not want to die. There is no way to sugar coat the word of God. The verse says that God did not tempt me and if I allow these temptations to become sin it will lead to death. Death in this verse means both spiritually and physically. Yes there is redemption, yes there is grace but contrary to popular belief grace is not to be used in vain. There is a clear distinction between sinning because you do not know right from wrong, and sinning despite knowing the facts. When we sin after we gain the knowledge of the Truth that, we are using God's grace in vain.

As God's co-workers we urge you not to receive God's grace in vain. 2 Corinthians 6:1 NIV

Instead of living like a people who do not know Christ, we are called to be different. To not do what our friends say is okay to do. I have gotten some of the worst advice from my friends. Thank God I did not follow all of it, but I realize now that the Lord was protecting me.

Do not get me wrong. I do not believe that having friendships with the opposite sex or boyfriends is wrong. I want to be married someday. Now I see how my life would be different if I was still dating one of my ex-boyfriends or got my way and married one of my old crushes because he had a nice smile and toned arms. I know that I would not be on the road that I am now running towards God at this speed.

I still have weak moments where I feel that I need to gain the attention from some male around me. The Lord quickly warns me or pulls me out of those situations. I firmly believe that my life path is marrying someone who loves God more than me. I now see that loving God should not be the only criteria and God will send someone with that and much more.

Drinking

You say, "I am allowed to do anything"--but not everything is good for you. You say, "I am allowed to do anything"--but not everything is beneficial.
1 Corinthians 10:23 NLT

I have no problem with people drinking. But I know that I cannot drink more than two or three drinks in any setting. On top of that, I have a strong conviction about drinking around certain groups of people, especially people that drink irresponsibly and men that I was either once attracted to or that I am attracted to now. If I have more than two or three drinks I get really flirty and as you can see from the previous section that leads to nothing but lustful, sinful thoughts. I learned that I am touchy and have thoughts that are not for the Lord. I know that I cannot drink. I am at the point in my life where I cannot compromise my spirituality for something as small as an overpriced mojito.

As I am around people that are drunk or a tipsy I realized that I honestly cannot be in negative environments like that. If people are drinking with the intention of getting drunk, I cannot be there. I can go to dinner where people are drinking with dinner and be okay. As I grow in the Lord, my threshold for certain activities gets lower and lower.

    I am telling you this not to change your mind about drinking but to get you to think about the things in your life that may be fine for some Christians to do, but that you cannot do. Some people cannot watch movies with a lot of profanity. I've met people that cannot listen to certain music. In order to live a life that is pure in every aspect we must find out what the Lord wants us to let go of to gain more of him. Everyone has things in their lives that they need to let go of that stops them from moving forward with their relationship with Christ.

I will not set my eyes on anything that is worthless
Psalm 101:3a ESV

    The Lord has shown me other areas of my life that are not sins, but that I can do without. I stop myself from sinning and from the extra baggage that I will just have to unload one day. Once I was watching a British television series and the Lord asked me to stop watching it. The show had a great story line and characters, but it was quite lewd at times. The extra aspects of the show made it unbeneficial for me to watch. Some followers of Christ could watch the show and have no reaction to it. I, on the other hand, cannot. I also had to cut excessive television from my life, in general. I realized while in high school that I get nothing done if I watch television. I used to waste hours of my time watching television. The Lord wants to protect me from putting images in my brain that He will just have to release from me later.

    The Lord made me self-reflective. Although discipline is not my strong suit, I realize quickly what in my life is distracting me from what the Lord wants me to do. Distractions hinder us from greatness. For me laziness (in the form of sleep), boys, friendships, my smart phone, certain television shows, and my horrible candy addiction distract me. When I realize these things, I quickly get rid of them. I still battle with laziness. I cannot figure out why this is so strong on my life. But time after time, the Lord helps me get my work done in time. The Lord reveals to me how these things are affecting my life spiritually. My health and school performance are affected when I do not make the right decisions about my life.

The Lord revealed how my laziness has affected my life. I went to the alter after church one day and just kept crying. I had no word for what I was going through. When the sweet lady praying for me and asked what I needed, I had no answer. I just cried. She told me that God said I had wastelands in my life. I was wasting time. I was idle for most of the summer of 2014 and did not work on any of the projects God gave me to do. God told me through the woman that I had to make a choice to walk where God wants me to or to stay idle. This was the first time in my life that I saw the direct spiritual effects of being lazy. A paper that did not get done or a phone call that I neglected to me did not have spiritual consequences, but it does. I believe that everything we do affects our spiritual selves, and I was making my spiritual self very lazy.

Grad School Ready?

My road to grad school started while I was applying to college as a senior in high school. I thought that I wanted to go to Dillard University and be either a veterinarian or psychologist. For some reason, I did not even apply to Dillard, and I am now neither a vet nor a psychologist. Nothing is wrong with Dillard University, nor is there anything wrong with being a vet or psychologist, but I know that I would have been a totally different person today if I went to that school and pursued those occupations. God guides every step of our paths if we allow him to guide.

The Lord changed my heart quickly. I applied to only two universities my senior year of high school, one of which was Xavier University of Louisiana. While attending Xavier University, I visited an office the Graduate Placement Office. There is not another office like it in the country. Not only was I a part of this office, but the beautiful people in the office saw enough in me to make me a Ronald E. McNair Scholar. Through this federally funded program, students from underrepresented populations that are given extra help in GRE prep, campus visitations, essay writing and overall mentorship to reach doctoral programs. This program and the staff of this office were a blessing from God. I would not know the first steps in getting to a doctoral program without the staff in this office and a few choice professors that believed in me.

I applied to many schools and Baylor University seemed to be the best fit for me. I quickly learned that the Lord did not have me here just to earn a degree, but to learn more about him and his power. On the days when graduate school is horrible and feels like it will never end, I remind myself that I am supposed to be here. I am supposed to learn both inside and outside the classroom. I go through cycles of asking God his plan for my life, and he tells me plainly to "finish your degree." In graduate school, I've learned so much. I am learning about the Holy Spirit, life with Jesus, and seeing God as my father.

Graduate school is my training ground. I have learned how to work with diverse groups of people. I have learned how to work statistical software. I have learned how to navigate the business world. I know that God has a mission for me and that I have to wait for him to show me how.

The Holy Spirit Guides

If you love me, obey my commandments. And I will ask the Father, and he will give you another Advocate, who will never leave you. He is the Holy Spirit, who leads into all truth. The world cannot receive him, because it isn't looking for him and doesn't recognize him. But you know him, because he lives with you now and later will be in you.
John 14:15-18 NLT

Towards the end of 2013, the Lord was preparing me to bring my husband into my life. The church did a six-week sermon series entitled, "Doing Your Season Well." The pastor touched on every stage of life: singleness, dating, marriage, children, etc. My lovely discipler felt like the Lord told her to talk to me about dating. One of my big brothers thought it was a good idea to go down a long list of men for me to date. An older lady I just met told me the story of how she met her husband at a volleyball game. For some reason, dating was coming up in random conversations with random people.

On the night of New Year's Eve, I was at a party put on by one of my best friends. I promised another friend that I would come to the party that she was throwing. The Holy Spirit asked my repeatedly as I left the first party, "Where are you going?" and he said, "You need to stay here." I got into my car to leave and I did not listen. I kept driving. At this party, I saw an old fling. I let him back into my life. Although nothing physical happened, it quickly became the most stressful six months of my life. I was praying about our relationship and I heard God say clearly, "You can be with him, but every plan I have for you will be harder to accomplish." As I stated earlier, I have a problem with men. No matter how cute I thought he was or how much he made me laugh, I knew that he was not the right one for me. He could not even pray for me if I needed him to. I knew that I did not want to live a life fighting with him over spiritual things. He would never understand them if he doesn't allow Jesus in his heart and be transformed. These are the moments I have to thank God for shaking me out of my flesh and drawing me back to him.

Because I was not obedient to the Holy Spirit on New Year's Eve, the Lord told me I had to wait before he allowed someone in my life. I wasn't sad. I wasn't mad. I felt anxious thinking about a man wanting to marry me and be with me for the rest of his life. So I think I needed the break.

I asked the Lord what I needed to learn while I wait. Me, not being God, thought it was to not talk to this individual anymore. The real reason was to be obedient to the Holy Spirit. God told me that I would speak in front of large crowds of people and that I needed to represent him well. In order for this to happen, I needed to listen more closely to the Holy Spirit.

The Holy Spirit is here for us to follow. The Holy Spirit is the second best gift from God besides Jesus. Holy Spirit will comfort us and guide us into the places where there is Truth.

The Holy Spirit has literally saved my life many times, spiritually and physically. Once when leaving school, I came to a four way stop sign. I was the only car at the stop and was about to drive forward but the Holy Spirit told me to wait. I waited a couple more seconds and a speeding car ran the stop sign to my right. The driver either did not know that there was a stop sign there or was not paying attention. The Holy Spirit saved me from harm. That was a testimony I wanted to share with everyone. Being obedient has its benefits.

Holy Desires

I look at people like Mother Teresa, or Martin Luther King Jr., or Gustavo Gutierrez and think how do I change the world like these people? Then I realize I actually want to improve the way Historically Black Colleges and Universities (HBCUs) educate our youth. I want to be a dean one day. I think there are still disparities in the ways that we are educated especially at some smaller schools that do not have large endowments. This is a big dream that I have. I think that this task is excessively large and that I will never be qualified to do it. When I have serious doubts of my skill set and capabilities the Lord reminds me that he put those desires in my heart. This means that he will give me the strength, knowledge, and wisdom to do what he wants me to do.

The Lord sends people in my life to speak to me at right the moments to pull me through. I was going through a low point in my life. I was questioning my path in life. Honestly, I was more afraid of achieving my dreams than of not achieving them. I feel really small and insignificant a lot of times. I feel like the Lord cannot possibly use someone like me to share his word and make significant changes in the world. During those times, someone prayed for me and told me that God put those desires in my heart for a reason. I knew at that moment if I stayed with Jesus that he would guide my steps into the greatness he has for me. I will have to follow him and him only.

God wants to do this for each and every one of us. He wants to give us all the desires that he placed in us.

Delight yourself in the LORD; And He will give you the desires of your heart.
Psalms 37:4 NASB

The most important part of the above verse is the beginning: "Delight yourself in the Lord." So many of us quote only half of the verse, we do not talk about how we must live in a way that is pleasing to God.

In addition to this desire, I have the desire to preach the gospel and see millions of people saved. My desire is to share his love with all people. Again, this is hard and scary. How am I supposed to go about doing this? Who gets invited to speak at world conferences? Does this mean I will be a preacher? A missionary? I get excited and scared as I type this. I do not know what my path will look like, but I will make myself available to God. I see that my life will be multi-faceted and that the

Lord will use me to lead people to him using different areas of my life.

The same is true for anyone reading this book, no matter how old you are, how many kids you have, what your bank account looks like, God has a plan and wants you to be a part of it.

Confession Moment

Therefore confess your sins to each other and pray for each other so that you may be healed. The prayer of a righteous person is powerful and effective.
James 5:16 NIV

To be honest, I did not want protection sometimes. I wanted to have sex, eat the candy, or be distracted and not finish this book. But my love for God quickly corrected me. I realize the closer I get to God that it is hard to turn back to those things that I once enjoyed. I realized that I will lose my way if I turn around. There is more to lose now than there were 5 years ago in my life. There are more people in my life now. I cannot let my flesh rule me, but rather let God rule my flesh.

Elevation Worship has a song that says, "Give my faith to trust what you say/That your good and your love is great/ I'm broken inside I give you my life." The chorus says, "I may be weak/But your spirit's strong in me/My flesh my fail/But my God you never will."

I am weak, but God is strong. I have so many fears and I realize that I operate more out of those fears rather than from my faith in God. I wanted to have sex because I know what sex is like. I did not know what it meant to have a relationship with a male that was not truly my friend without it. I wanted to not finish this book because I am afraid of what other people will say about me or about my life. I can no longer make choices out of my weaknesses but rather out of His strength.

I have absolutely no idea where I will be in 5, 10, or 30 years from now, but I know that the Lord will be with me and everything will be all right. The Lord always shows up in my life when I need him. His word says that he will give us a way out of temptation, and he does just that. God is always trying to protect me as a good father should.

I pray that you are able to see how the Lord has guided your life and protected you. Even though you do not see him, God is there watching, and guiding. God is always trying to talk to us. He always wants to share his love or plan for our lives with us. We must be willing to obey him and receive protection from the outside world.

But if we confess our sins to him, he is faithful and just to forgive us our sins and to cleanse us from all wickedness 1 John 1:9 NLT

Guidance in your life

"Your beliefs don't make you a better person, your behavior does"

God has great plans for us all. We are all to live a life that draws men to him. If we allow him to, he will protect us from harm and evil that may stop us from completing his task. I want his love for you to reflect in your life. Take time to ask God what he has for your life.

Ask the Holy Spirit to bring to your memory some events and times that, you may not have been aware of.

How is the Lord protecting you?

What is he protecting you from?

What is he protecting you for?

It is important to remember that there are times we will go through things because that is how God works. He allows trials and tests in our lives. He uses experiences to help us grow. But as his child, he also wants to protect us from harm that we might put ourselves through.

When has God allowed you to go through things to make you better?

What came out of those times?

Do you see God in those times?

Remember most importantly that God is the reason that you are here and he has a plan for you to change the world, one person at a time.

4 prayer is powerful

Pray without ceasing. 1 Thessalonians 5:17 KJV

Life never stands still. We are constantly changing. God is waiting for us to realize that we need him in every step we take; literally every breath we take is from him. Sometimes, like in me, God takes everything we have from us to show us his power.

The Lord took from me everything I relied on; everything and everyone I used to deceive myself. The man I knew I was going to marry, my vanity, and school coming easy was all taken away.

It had gotten to be too much for me to bear. All I could do was get out of my bed one night during my sophomore year of college and literally cry out to God for hours. I cried, and cried, and cried. I only recently think about the people in my dorm and what they thought was going on inside of my room. I was so immersed in the presence of the Lord to care at the time. God shattered the reality I knew. My reality without him was longer valuable. I had to find value in him. I had to find truth in him. I had to find life in him. I had to find him.

This low point in my life led me to the conclusion that I needed to learn how to pray and talk to God. I wanted more of him. I wanted more of him to fill me. I knew that he was the only thing that would satisfy the holes in my heart. Nevertheless, I did not know where to start praying. I grew up in church my entire life but did not know how to go to God on my own and pray for help.

The Lord's Prayer

Years after this dorm room experience, I still did not really know how to pray to God. I was journaling, but I wanted more- much more. In order to learn about prayer, I read books and asked my mother and others. Eventually I concluded that I needed to study how Jesus prayed because he is the model. I decided to look at what we have come to know as the Lord's Prayer. I read the Matthew 6:9-13 version over and over.

After this manner therefore pray ye: Our Father which art in heaven, Hallowed be thy name. Thy kingdom come, Thy will be done in earth, as it is in heaven. Give us this day our daily bread. And forgive us our debts, as we forgive our debtors. And lead us not into temptation, but deliver us from evil: For thine is the kingdom, and the power, and the glory, for ever. Amen.
Matthew 6:9-13 KJV

Even after this, I failed miserably. All I did was read it over and over and attempt to break it down verse by verse. I did learn to trust God for my daily bread and for true forgiveness from my sin. At this point, I did not know how to ask the Lord questions about the Bible. I actually did not even know you could do that. So again I felt defeated in my prayer life. I was thinking excessively about it. I thought that there was a secret formula, that I could break the code. As I look back on this time, I see how God's grace covered me because I was running toward him.

Who is God?

After the Lord's Prayer study session, I realized that I had no idea who God is really. Not that I would ever understand the fullness of him, but I just did not understand what it meant to talk to him because I did not know who he was. I remembered my favorite Old Testament verse:

God said to Moses, "I AM WHO I AM. This is what you are to say to the Israelites: 'I AM has sent me to you.'"
Exodus 3:14 NIV

Moses asked God, "Who do I tell the Israelites sent me?" In this verse, Moses was looking for a specific name or person to tell the Israelites when they questioned his legitimacy to free them from Pharaoh's capture. God's answer was perfect, as usual. For me it means to never put God in a box. He is who he is. He will forever fill any role that he needs to. For the Israelites, he was their deliverer and savior at that time.

I think of this verse often. I find myself in situations where I only know to call Jesus and tell him that I need him to show up. This happens in interactions with others and when I am alone. I see that God is real because he always comes through. There has never been a moment in my life where God has not shown up in the situation in order for me to triumph. This triumph often came after a lesson from God.

As I grow in the Lord, I come to see the relationship of God the Father, Jesus the Son, and the Holy Spirit differently. All three are divine and help me through life, yet there is only one God. Each one plays a special role in my life and I have different relationships with each member. They are three distinct people, yet they are one and come from the source of God the Father.

God does not fit into a box. I knew that God created the world. He sent his son to earth to die for our sins. Lastly, he left the Holy Spirit to guide us. God, Jesus, and Holy Spirit then started taking other roles in my life and started showing me who they are. One of the hardest relationships for me to accept was God as my Father. I could never bring myself to say it. The Holy Spirit exposed the source of this struggle to me. The reason I had trouble calling God my father was because of the imperfect father that I have here on earth. (We all have imperfect fathers and mothers because they are humans.) I learned three things as I worked through this with God. First, all people are imperfect but how we react to them is on us. Second, my father did what he knew how to do as a father and is great at it. Lastly, the Lord showed me that so many other people could not come to God as their father in prayer because of their imperfect earthly fathers. So many people are searching for fathers that they can rely on and will not abandoned them. God is the Perfect Father. This is hard to acknowledge when our only reference to a father is the one we have on earth. I have gotten over this hurdle and pray often that all people are able to see God as their father no matter what type of earthly father they have.

After finding God as my father, I came to know Jesus as my friend. I had a vision of Jesus and I sitting on a beach next to one another. I love the beach. I would be a beach bum if I lived near the ocean. I think this is why Jesus and me were on a beach in this vision.

There are so many times when I need comfort. I have visions of him holding my hands or my head on His shoulder. This vision is the way I communicate with Jesus to know how close I am to him. I am most happy when I am sitting next to him on that beach. The best feeling in the world is when the Lord tells me that he is proud of me. These feelings only come when I am close to him and obey what he tells me to do. I ask Jesus to show me how close we are through these visions. Once, he showed me standing up with my back to Him. This was such a reality check. I knew that I was not living the way I should be, but I did not care. Jesus was faithful enough to show me where I was in life and was patient enough to let me correct it. This vision is one I want to carry with me throughout life.

Jesus and I truly are friends. I feel like there were and still are many times God wanted to correct me but Jesus saved me from the punishment. I am so thankful to have a friend like Jesus that would take time to save me from punishment. Like a true earthly friend he gives me direction and sacrificed for me.

Jesus is my savior. When I look at my life and how I have changed and grown to know the Lord, I realize that this is all because of Jesus. He is the reason that I am free enough today to even tell others about my disgraceful past. Jesus died the most horrific and dishonorable death of his time for my sins. He died to save me from the wrath of hell for my "big" sins and my "small" ones. He died to give me a chance at life. He died so that I can walk with him one day hand in hand. He died to wipe away all fear, insecurities, and all inner warfare. He died most importantly because He loves us.

I am forever indebted to Him.

Jesus left the earth after his resurrection but left the Holy Spirit to dwell and live among us. The Holy Spirit became my guide over the years. It was hard for me be obedient to anyone. I have bluntly disobeyed teachers, my parents, and any authority figure in my life, even God. The Holy Spirit is so gentle with me and tells me when to turn around, not answer the phone, or not say anything rude to the people around me. I am very rebellious, but the Holy Spirit will not allow me to stay that way. The Holy Spirit corrects me both in earthly ways and in spiritual ways. The Holy Spirit is my helper. I feel his presence when I am praying and he guides my day if I allow him to. I personally dedicated 2014 to becoming a better listener and to be more obedient to the Holy Spirit. I became too afraid of man for a time to listen to Holy Spirit, but now I am back on the right track. Man cannot save me from Hell; Jesus has already done that for me.

The only way to be obedient is to know God's voice. I am learning the difference between God's voice and my own selfishness. The more we pray, the more we can distinguish his voice from our own and from the enemy's.

So... How do I pray?

After I figured out better who God was, I still did not know how to pray in a way in which I was satisfied. When I moved to Waco, I saw people praying in different ways that I had never seen before. I used to journal, but I moved to a church where I saw people offer worship and pray in different ways. I have seen people literally lay on the ground unable to move because the presence of the

Lord was so strong.

After this, I realized that there is no specific way to pray. There is no formula. That the low experience I had my sophomore year of college was me praying. Journaling is prayer. Talking out loud to God is prayer. I was not lost as I originally thought. As long as I was being sincere when I talked to the Lord, everything would be okay. The only thing constant in my prayer life was that I was attempting to pray without ceasing.

Rejoice evermore. Pray without ceasing. In every thing give thanks: for this is the will of God in Christ Jesus concerning you. 1 Thessalonians 5:16-18 KJV

As I got more comfortable in prayer with the Lord, He asked me to do things in prayer and even in worship that I was uncomfortable with. The Lord asked me to jump while in prayer. I hate jumping, with a passion. I see no point of jumping in any setting, whether that be in exercise, in worship, or in prayer. But I was obedient and did what he asked of me. Every time I pray and he asks me to do something I am uncomfortable with, I get break through. I see now that the Lord wants us to be uncomfortable. That is where our weakness comes to the forefront and his strength takes over. We are to live in his strength not in our weaknesses.

My prayer time has changed as my stages of my life have changed. I rarely journal anymore, but that does not mean that I will not in three months or that my prayer time is any less effective. We have to figure out what the Lord wants us to do. I had to figure how he wanted to communicate with me. Currently, I am sitting on the floor in the middle of my bedroom. I am laying on a hardwood floor and it's cold, but I do what the Lord has told me to do.

No matter how I pray, I know that I must not only ask, but listen. Listening is the part of prayer that I am horrible at. I talk to God and tell him all of my problems and ask questions, but don't take time to listen to his answer. It is a little crazy for me to do this. How can I ask a question of God and not take the time to wait for the answer? I have even fallen asleep during my quiet time with God. I try to have prayer before I start my day, and most times, I am still half asleep. I am quite pitiful sometimes. But I am learning how to be a better listener. The Lord wants my best in everything. Falling asleep during prayer is not my best.

Prayer is Humbling

As I mentioned earlier, I was one of the most prideful people in the world. Smart, funny, and cute. What else could someone want in a friend, daughter, and a mate? That is how I used to think. How silly of me? Thank God for grace and revelation that I am nothing without him.

The Word of God says: *If anyone thinks he is something when he is nothing, he deceives himself.*
Galatians 6:3 NIV.

The closer I got to God, the more I realized that I was only deceiving myself. I thought way too much of myself to be used by him. It is as if I did not need him. This is one of the most dangerous states of mind to have. I had a friend to tell me his successes were because of the things he did. He said that God did not help him at all. I was shocked and had absolutely no way to explain to him that he could have dropped dead right in the moment if the Lord wanted to, but His grace is the reason that we keep breathing.

The most humbling thing about prayer is learning not to trust in superficial things that will fade anyway. I can say that I am the best at this sport or the best at that skill, but when I die, will it matter? The life I live on earth is short and will end soon. I know that I must begin to build my home in heaven. We all have gifts to use on earth, but ultimately our gifts are not about us. They are for adding souls to God's kingdom. This is humbling. My ability to preach is not for me to show people that I know the Bible, but rather to show that God is true and to encourage individuals to find Him.

I am humbled at how small I am in comparison to God. I have learned not to compare myself to others, but rather to Jesus. Jesus is the measurement. When I do this, I truly see how I always fall short, how I need God to stand in my gap.

But God chose the foolish things of the world to shame the wise; God chose the weak things of the world to shame the strong. I Corinthians 1:27 NIV

Let us not be the people that God must put to shame, but rather humble ourselves to be the people God will use to shame others into repentance.

In the humbling process, I am honored. The fact that God would use someone as screwed up as myself to add people to His kingdom is honoring. Being honored by God is so much more satisfying than any honor from humans that I think I have "earned" things on my own to date.

Sacrifices in Prayer

You would not be pleased with sacrifices, or I would bring them. If I brought you a burnt offering, you would not accept it. The sacrifice you want is a broken spirit. A broken and repentant heart, O God, you will not despise. Look with favor on Zion and help her; rebuild the walls of Jerusalem. Then you will be pleased with worthy sacrifices and with our whole burnt offerings; and bulls will again be sacrificed on your altar.
Psalm 51:16-19 NIV

I wanted my prayer life to be different. I grew up hearing the same exact prayers every Sunday. I knew what they were going to say before they said it. As I moved to New Orleans and then Waco, I learned two new sets of clichés. I could not bear to hear them. Not every cliché was biblically based and some made absolutely no sense at all. I grew to hate clichés after God showed me that I was not living what the Bible said, but rather the clichés I had become accustomed to. I was so obsessed with not using by clichés that I would never say them in prayer and even rebuked myself when I thought them.

I want all the sacrifices I bring to be accepted by God. I do not want to waste the time God has given me. This was even included in what I sacrificed to him in prayer. There were so many times I went through the motions of prayer without actually praying. If a prayer "worked" for someone else, (meaning that God gave them what they asked) I would pray the same exact thing expecting the same results. God is not a robot that produces the same products if we push the right buttons.

These prayers were not from a broken spirit, but rather me trying to get exactly what I wanted from God.

If someone told me the prayer they spoke to gain the strength to lose weight, I would pray the same prayer (and not do the work) and expect the same results. This cycle would repeat with anything I wanted or thought I needed. He showed me that I could communicate with Him and ask for what I want sincerely without the help of anymore else. God reminded me that I am an original. My prayers can be different. Furthermore, I actually did not want the same results as the other people. I wanted my own personalized prayers answered from God.

The Bible tells us to sometimes to sacrifice through fasting. Fasting occurs when we restrain ourselves from physical things for spiritual gain. Most people fast from food, but television and social media can be good fasts too. I failed at fasts. I failed everyone I tried until the Lent season of 2015. This does not change the call on our lives to fast and pray. One reason I never completed fast because I rarely get with the mission of the fast. I usually just do them either because the church I am going to at the time is doing it, or because I want something from God.

The first reason is not a bad reason to fast. I believe in a church fasting together to see changes within the church. There is also nothing wrong with the second reason of fasting. It is okay to fast to show God that you are serious about what you are asking for. For me though, the sacrifice was not real. During those church-wide fasts, I just wanted to show the church how good of a Christian I was. As for the fast I did for myself, I just wanted something very selfish from God. I thought for a time that God was similar to a gumball machine. I give him a little of a sacrifice and he gives me a quick reward. I am learning the God does not grant wishes. If we sacrifice for Him and truly love the people he has put in our lives for us to love, he will give us so much more in purity, peace, and his spirit.

Real Conversations

I have insecurities. I compare myself to others all of the time. I looked, and to be honest, still look at what they are doing for Christ. I would say I am just volunteering with this group or I am just in graduate school writing papers while people are out there producing music, preaching the gospel, speaking at conferences. Why am I just sitting here chilling? As I complain in prayer, which I often do, the Lord reminds me that my path is mine. He did not create me for those things or to do them at that this time. I need more preparation, more stamina, and most importantly more of him. But God has me right where he wants me. I am to be here learning and growing from him and his people.

Honestly, this sucks sometimes. But the Bible doesn't say that life will be flowers and fairies, but rather that our burdens would be light.

Then Jesus said, "Come to me, all of you who are weary and carry heavy burdens, and I will give you rest. Take my yoke upon you. Let me teach you, because I am humble and gentle at heart, and you will find rest for your souls. For my yoke is easy to bear, and the burden I give you is light." Matthew 11:28-30 NLT

I can truly say if I follow that path the Lord has for

me, then my burdens are light. When I attempt to pick up issues and situations myself, problems arise. The burden gets way too heavy for me and I have to give them right back to him. The worst part about this is that I either end up five steps further back than I was before, or right where I left off in my growth towards God.

My relationship with God is what got me to these real conversations with him. Think about it, the more comfortable you are with your friends, the more you tell them. The more they correct you, the more you are open with them. The same is true with God. He will give us more of his realness and correction, as we get closer to him. I was truly a child in my walk with him for quite some time. Then I grew up. The Lord knew he could trust me with more wisdom and with more of his power.

The Lord asked me once in prayer, "What are you doing?!"

I had to answer him. This was one of the most embarrassing moments in my life. I knew that the situation I put myself in was not conducive to kingdom building, that all parties involved would eventually crash and burn if I did not stop the train where it was. Wake up calls like these occur often when I pray. They are both embarrassing and rewarding because I am able to see how God genuinely cares about me.

With more realness, wisdom, and power came more responsibility. God showed me how my choices affect those around me. I am learning that God is real when he speaks. He has been direct with me during prayer and throughout my days with him. I have learned that he cares more than I could ever imagine, and that I need to get over that. He will not let me get by with doing wrong. But rather correct me gently using the Holy Spirit as my guide.

Correction happens in prayer

Through these real conversations, the Lord corrects me. The Lord shows me two important things in prayer: who I am, and how to be more like him. In the last few years, He is teaching me that my words matter. Many things that I have said about others have come true. I should not have said them, I should not have even thought of them. When people repeat my words back to me I realize how sharp my words are, and God is still changing that in me.

I say things without thinking most times because I am not serious. Others often think that I am serious and run with the words that I say. One of my aunts thinks that I am depressed and distraught because of the words that I said. We went to the dinner table and I was saying that I believe that my brother is everyone's favorite and that I was just the child everyone puts up with. I can see how my aunt would have thought I really believed this and lived my life through it. I joke a lot but the Lord is showing me why it is important to choose my words wisely.

When it comes to exercising, I say that I cannot do certain movements. Often this is not the case. The Lord has shown me that I say things, and they become real. I say, "I cannot do a bear crawl," so therefore I cannot do it. The times I try and things happen I see how my words that affect my attitude really matter. The days that I change my attitude towards the workout are the days that I get more out of it and am able to burn more calories.

I now see that I need to be more careful with the words that come out of my life because they effect those around me, sometimes more than they affect me.

Prayer reminds of purpose

I, like every other person in the world, have been disappointed many times by people that I am close to. Like others, I have had people promise me things never to give them or bring up the fact that they harmed me. I have had meetings called to discuss the issues people have with me and only me. In fact, there was a meeting where everyone there told me the problems they had with me. It was crazy, and in my opinion, should have never happened. People have gossiped about me and broken my trust, and ruined a friendship that I had. I have been the topic of bashing sessions with no one there to save me. A lot of crazy stuff has happened to me.

I used to hold on to these moments in life. I attempted to use the hurt as ammunition to hurt others. But the Lord showed me how to be more focused on him and what he has to give me in exchange for the stuff that I held on to. I realized that I could hold on to his peace, peace that never left my side. He has shown me that I can hold on to his unending joy. Through every situation, I see how the Lord has held my hand and how I have come out on the other side.

I do not believe that everything happens for a reason, but that there is a lesson to learn in every season. I have learned so many lessons in friendships. I have learned how to be more loving. I truly try to love like Jesus does. God has shown me that my purpose in life has not changed because of the situations I have experienced.

So many times, I pray for things that I forget I prayed for. Still the Lord gives them to me, but not before, I take time in prayer to be changed. I have big dreams for my life. I know that the Lord is ready to give them to me if I only stay in prayer mode. It is really the only mode to be in.

I value when people are genuine with me. So when I am fake with God it shows up in what I produce for him. He has shown me that I must be real with him about my fears and failure for him to show me how he will use these things for his glory.

Boldness in Prayer

One day Moses said to the Lord, "You have been telling me, 'Take these people up to the Promised Land.' But you haven't told me whom you will send with me. You have told me, 'I know you by name, and I look favorably on you.' If it is true that you look favorably on me, let me know your ways so I may understand you more fully and continue to enjoy your favor. And remember that this nation is your very own people." Exodus 33:12-13 NLT

The Lord wants us to ask for things from him. I have missed so many opportunities because I was afraid to ask God. I am reading Exodus and realized that Moses was one of the boldest characters in the Bible. Not because he led the people out of Egypt, but because he asked Yahweh for what he needed. Not only did Moses ask for what he needed, Moses reminded the Lord regularly of what He promised Moses and the Israelites. Take the verse above for example, the Moses said, "If it is true." That's like me saying, "God if you are sure this is what you want, then..." It takes some boldness to remind God of what he said even if it is in a gentle manner. Lastly, Moses asked for mercy over his people for their disobedience. He saved them from God's wrath so many times. I cannot fathom being this bold with God. "We're doomed. God's wrath is going to wipe us out tonight and we just have to deal with it" This is closer to what I would have said. But Moses did not do that. He called on the Lord and even asked for more from him.

Moses immediately threw himself to the ground and worshiped. And he said, "O Lord, if it is true that I have found favor with you, and then please travel with us. Yes, this is a stubborn and rebellious people, but please forgive our iniquity and our sins. Claim us as your own special possession." Exodus 34:8-9 NLT

God has taught me that he is my father, but also that Jesus is my friend and the Holy Spirit is there to help me. So when I am afraid to go to God directly, I can ask one of the other two to do it for me. Praise God for Jesus! One day I will be strong enough to go directly to God when asking for things. A part of the reason that I am so afraid is because I believe that I am unworthy, which is absolutely true. I have done nothing for the Lord to reward me. But He does anyways.

The Lord has showed me many times in prayer that I miss things because I am not bold enough to ask. Once I asked God why I did not get to go on a summer trip that all of my friends went on, and he told me, "You did not ask." I was shocked The Lord knew that I wanted these things, but because I was not bold enough to ask, I did not receive them. Using Moses as an example, he asked to understand God more fully and to continue to have favor in his sight. A consistent prayer life will have you asking for things that you would not normally ask for. You ask God for supernatural things that only he could provide. God wants us to ask for supernatural things from him. He operates in the supernatural. I am in the process not asking for earthly surface-level things, but to be bold and ask for supernatural things that only he can do.

There were so many other bold people in the Bible that I look up to. The Lord told me I am like Esther. At this point in my life, I had read the book of Esther, but I had to read it again. The book is about Esther, a Jew and a Queen, saving all of the Jewish people in the kingdom from mass murder. In Chapter 4:16 Esther says:

"Go, gather together all the Jews who are in Susa, and fast for me. Do not eat or drink for three days, night or day. I and my attendants will fast as you do. When this is done, I will go to the king, even though it is against the law. And if I perish, I perish." Esther 4:16NIV

After I read this verse, I first prayed that I would have the boldness Esther had. Then I read it again and asked God, "Are you sure that I am like Esther?" I do not know if I am willing to die because of any cause to be honest. But deep down, I know that I, if the Lord called me to lay down my life physically until death, would do it. This is crazy because I will not always talk to someone about

Christ or complete a fast, but I know that I will profess him if someone threatens my life. I am somewhat of an extremist. Esther was a woman who was bold and obedient. In order to be more of both of these things I must pray. Pray continually to stay in the spirit of God.

The good news is Esther does not die when she talks to the king and all the Jews in the kingdom are saved!

Self- Control

Self-control is a fruit of the spirit.

But the fruit of the Spirit is love, joy, peace, longsuffering, kindness, goodness, faithfulness, gentleness, self-control; against such there is no law. Galatians 5:22-23 KJV

Self-control is needed to live a Christ-like life and we have access to it because of the Holy Spirit. As of late I have not been having self-control. I am an addict as I stated earlier. I am addicted to candy. Science has proven that we can be addicted to refined sugar like any other drug. Some fast food restaurants even put sugar on their fries in order for you to return to that fast food restaurant. I really have an issue. I will eat candy over a meal and used to buy candy every time I went into a store. My friends try to intervene when I am eating candy, but it does not help. I always find a way to eat it. God has even talked to me before I take my first bite, He tells me that I do not need it and that I have power over it. I still chose the candy. I want to get better. I've gotten prayer for this addiction; it's a real thing. There is no nutritional value in it and I do want my future children to struggle with candy addiction like I do.

In addition, I was once addicted to buying clothes. The clothes addiction is one that I am ashamed to admit because I would buy a new pair of shoes or a new shirt when I know that I cannot afford it. I am not being responsible with the money God has given me. There were numerous times in college when I have had to tell my parents that I had no money because I spent my last dollar on a pair of shoes or a purse. This is not a fruitful life. The Lord did not want me to live this way.

As an introspective person, I am usually aware of the patterns in my life. My addictive patterns disappear when I have a consistent prayer life. If I am not consistent, I have less self-control. When I go to my Father daily with issues and get guidance, I am able to function more disciplined and God honoring. Prayer works!

I am more productive in school and at work when I have prayed. Now that my prayer life is more consistent, when I do not pray I get unbalanced. The Lord has shown me that I need him to focus. One week at school, I let my impulses or (lack of self-control) rule me. I allowed the fact that I wanted to watch a television series over homework. I allowed a friend who wanted to have lunch rule me instead of spending time writing a paper. I allowed the pretty day God created to take over instead of praying to God for strength for that day. In the last scenario, the Lord told me that he would give me other pretty days to enjoy. I still did not listen. I wanted to enjoy the day instead of sitting in my room.

God wants us to have self-control in all areas. I know

I am not being a good steward over my body if I consume too much candy. I am not a good steward of my money when I spend excessively on shoes that I do not need. The Lord literally lends us time and space to use while we are on this earth. We are wasting his time and his money when we do not have self-control.

As I sit currently with a new pair of boots, I debated on whether I should keep them or not. I have wrestled with my flesh and my spirit for about a week about them. The lack of peace within me probably means that I should take them back. (I returned them.) Again, the Holy Spirit guides and will not allow me to live in a sinful place. For me, buying boots that I do not need is sin. It means that I am living in excess. The Lord wants me to live in self-control and not be wasteful of His resources. (I bought them later again when they were on sale and I was at peace.)

> *But Samuel replied, "What is more pleasing to the LORD: your burnt offerings and sacrifices or your obedience to his voice? Listen! Obedience is better than sacrifice, and submission is better than offering the fat of rams.*
> 1 Samuel 15: 22 NLT

In the above verse, Samuel is telling his people that it is better to obey God in the first place than doing what you want and give God an offering for your sins. I used to live by the mantra: Ask for forgiveness, not permission. This is clearly opposite of what the Word instructs us to do.

The Lord has a way of guiding us to what is right and what is wrong in a gentle way. I knew I did not have the money when I swiped my debit card, but I did it anyway. Obedience is (way) better than sacrifice. Although taking back a pair of shoes is not that big of a deal, I will have to drive to the other side of town to do so. I will have to take time to make a trip to a place that I rarely go. Without the boots, I would have avoided this situation.

The same is true for the candy and me. I know that candy has no nutritional value. Because I have not filled my body with the proper nutrients, I am not the most prepared to work out. I have to stop jogging because I was light-headed. Candy will not give me the fuel to work out at my maximum level.

For me, self-control has, and is currently, shaping the way I think. It is all about wants and needs for me. I know that I do not *need* that skirt and candy. I *want* them both. No one will notice that I do not have that one pair of shoes that I skipped. My body unquestionably thanks me for not putting empty calories in it. God wants us to go to him with our wants and needs, but I am learning to not ask for wants that will eventually harm me. Lack of self-control is the reason why I have not completed a fast that lasts more than a day. The Lord is showing me that I do not need to rely on food; my strength can come from him.

Prayer is Healing-Let us stay free

O LORD my God, I called to you for help and you healed me. Psalm 30:2 ESV

Healing from so many emotional dysfunctions because of prayer: the scars of past relationships, the badly worded statements from my mother, or the way my professor treated me. God helped me to see my role in each situation: How I contributed to the break down in the relationship. Also, he has comforted me and shown me how I can learn and grow from the situation.

God has shown me that he is the only person that can truly heal us. Every hole in my heart is partially and temporarily filled by earthly pleasures, but it will not be fully satisfied until God fills it. When I take the hurts of my heart to God, he takes them away. He does not remind me of who or what hurt me. He gives me something so much better in return. I have learned to rely on him for help in all situations where I can be hurt.

So Christ has truly set us free. Now make sure that you stay free, and don't get tied up again in slavery to the law. Galatians 5:1."NLT

God has shown me how I actually have reminded myself of the hurt. He has told me that I will continually hurt about certain situations until I give them totally to him. I have dealt with some of the same hurts for years because I either wore them as a badge or was afraid to let them go. Some people wear their hurts like a badge. They say and think things like, "I have been through too much to forgive them." They might say, "Look at all I've gone through to make it to where I am today."

When I finally gave my hurts to God, he healed me quickly. I never had to think about the crazy boy or how I felt after injustices happened to me. My pastor once said people that truly follow Jesus do not get offended. When you think about it, this must be true. I cannot be offended when I do not care about the people that live in this world with me. This is one of my many goals in life.

Then they cried to the LORD in their trouble, and he saved them from their distress. He sent forth his word and healed them; he rescued them from the grave. Let them give thanks to the LORD for his unfailing love and his wonderful deeds for men. Psalm 107:19-21 NIV

Friends and family members have all been a part of my hurt. I know that I cannot get mad at them for being themselves and not truly understanding me. I have a part to play in disputes with others. God shows me where I go wrong, how He still loves me, and how I am to love others in the same way.

I have loved you even as the Father has loved me. Remain in my love. When you obey my commandments, you remain in my love, just as I obey my Father's commandments and remain in his love. I have told you these things so that you will be filled with my joy. Yes, your joy will overflow! This is my commandment: Love each other in the same way I have loved you.
John 15:9-12 NLT

Praying Supernaturally

I indeed baptize you with water unto repentance: but he that cometh after me is mightier than I, whose shoes I am not worthy to bear: he shall baptize you with the Holy Ghost, and with fire: Matthew 3:11 KJV

While in undergrad, I met a Christian girl that tried to get me to understand and use the gift of tongues. I was not against the gift of tongues but was not ready to receive the gift at the time no matter how much she pressured me into doing so. I do not like to do stuff just because other people tell me to. I like to research and form my own conclusions. I knew that the gift of tongues was from God, but did not know how it worked.

At one point in my life, the Holy Spirit used to take over me and make me pray aloud in front of crowds of people, and I could not stop my mouth from moving. I knew it was supernatural and what the Lord wanted the congregation to hear at the time. These were surreal moments in my life that I did not quite understand was happening, but I knew it was God working inside of me.

At some point, I got the hang of praying, maybe. I realized that it did not have to be that hard, and that I could do it on a consistent basis. One day during lifegroup, we were talking about spiritual gifts. In the conversation, the gift of tongues came up. One of my close friends was talking about her experience with receiving the gift of tongues and the benefits of having this gift. I heard the Holy Spirit say, "I want that for you." I was never afraid of receiving the gift of tongues; I just never knew the purpose. I was not totally ready to receive that from God. The Holy Spirit kept saying, "I want that for you."

As I stated earlier, I am not the type of person that goes into the unknown easily. The same was true for the gift of tongues. I could not accept this gift during undergrad because I did not totally understand it. I had not done enough reading on it up until this point. The Lord knew that I was ready and kept telling me this during the lifegroup meeting.

I told my lifegroup leaders at the time what I heard

the Lord say. They immediately instructed me to go into another room where all the women in the group prayed over me, and I received the gift. It was amazing. It was interesting. It was different.

Like most other gifts given the by the Lord, the gift of tongues can be developed over time. That first night I felt like I only said two words. Now I pray for people and in my quiet time with this gift.

The gift of tongues is how I ask for things supernaturally. Sometimes I do not have words to say to God. I do not know what to ask for or how to ask it. In those times I use my gift. The Lord has shown me that it is a tool for his glory. I am to use this gift to lift him up and show others that he is real.

When I have absolutely no words to say when I pray for people, I pray in tongues to myself. I know that the Holy Spirit can cleanse or heal people with more power than I have. The gift of tongues has been a prayer saver for me many times throughout my life. I also have a one-track mind. There are many times when people will request that everyone pray aloud at the same time. I cannot pray aloud while others are. I begin to pray in tongues to allow for the Holy Spirit to take control instead.

The gift of tongues is something I treasure from the Lord and thank him for.

I know that he wants others to experience all the gifts that he is waiting to give to us.

Here is my personal understanding of the gift of

tongues (ask God and other spiritual leaders for more explanation). The Bible talks about believers being baptized in water and in spirit. They are two different things that can happen at two different times. When someone is baptized in water, they are born again as a new person. When someone is baptized in the Spirit, the Holy Spirit now lives inside of him or her. When someone is baptized in the Spirit, there are signs and gifts that come along with it. The Bible talks about the gift of tongues most, but there are others. The gift of tongues is the ability to speak in a heavenly language that only God or people with the gift of interpretation can understand. When he gives a message to a big group of people, there must be an interpreter to explain what the message was from the Lord.

When I first received the gift of tongues, it was scary because I often did not know what I was saying. The Holy Spirit took over. I discovered after a while that I would sometimes speak Spanish or the same words over and over. God is helping me to understand the power that comes along with this gift. I pray that you to understand this gift as well as the other gifts he gives.

Prayer is Life

Pray in the Spirit at all times and on every occasion. Stay alert and be persistent in your prayers for all believers everywhere. Ephesians 6:18 NLT

Prayer is simply a conversation with God.

Don't worry about anything; instead, pray about everything. Tell God what you need, and thank him for all he has done. Phil 4: 6 NLT

The verse above tells us what to say in our conversations with God. We should tell him what we need and thank him for what he has done. This is the more simple way to start a prayer life with God.

We should pray every day. It is our way to communicate with God. I do not do this every day. I have had so many distractions that stop me from living the life I want to live. I know the importance and I know how God desires this communication with me as his child. This does not make it any easier to pray every day and to not forget to live a life that follows God's plan.

I want to live my life in prayer. I know people that pray about everything. These people pray about what to wear to work on a normal day, whether to order beef or chicken at the wedding, or even how to style their hair that day. I used to think, "It does not take all of that." Now I see that God does care about every aspect of our lives. I realized that we could and should ask him for direction in every area of our lives. I do not know if I will ever ask God, "Should I order beef or chicken at this wedding," but I know this is an option for my life.

The Lord has taught me how to love through prayer, how to truly love others, and show them his kindness. It feels like every question I have about what to say to someone or what I should do with them ends with God saying, "To love them." Prayer was the life of Jesus. Love wp as the life of Jesus.

How can your prayer life be changed?

If we are to look like Christ, we are to learn how to pray like Christ. God calls us deeper into prayer with him. I want to be able to reach him more and more during the time I spend with him on a daily basis. God is looking for followers that will move toward praying consistently to him about our lives and on behalf of others.

I believe that everything is a process. In order to build a better prayer life, we should start by praying. Prayer is simply communicating with God. In effective communication you must both talk and listen. Listening is usually more important than talking in day to day conversation and the same is true with our relationship with God. We must listen to him to learn and grow.

The easiest way to practice is by waking up five minutes earlier and let God be the first person you talk to in the mornings. There are some days where I hit the snooze button one too many times and cannot do this but I strive to let this happen. If early mornings do not work for you, maybe you set a specific time during the day to spend with Jesus.

If you do not know what to pray about you can pray the Psalms, for the people you live with, or about a particular reoccurring situation in your life. Pray every There is always something to go to God for in prayer.

We should build up to the point where we are walking with the Holy Spirit all day. We ask and he responds, and he asks something of us and we respond.

Below are a few reflection questions to push forward your prayer life:

First reflect, am I truly connecting with God during my prayer times? If not, are there new places or times I can pray? The Lord wants to meet with you, he wants you to be in a place where you can meet him.

Are there times in my day in which I can stop and have prayer time?

If you are struggling to have daily prayer, are there any people in your life that can keep you accountable to pray?

As an exercise attempt to pray for three days straight without asking God for anything. This will help you see that prayer is more than asking God for things but rather communicating with him about who he is and on behalf of others. You can worship him and repent sins as well.

In order to improve our prayer lives. We must pray. This is the simplest thing for us to do.

conclusion: God is a God of action

If you are not someone who follows Christ my prayer is that you will read this book and see that no one who professes to know Christ is perfect. We all have fallen and need God to help us back up.

I pray that you grow to learn who Christ is. You will see that there was a purpose for his life and a purpose for his death. I pray that any unworthy thoughts you have towards forgiveness are wiped away. I pray you see that you forgiveness and the Lord are waiting to do this for you.

Now that you have read parts of my story (which I appreciate!), what does this have to do with you?

Find your passion and use it for Christ. Let no one tell you what you can and cannot do for Christ. If the Lord says do it, do it. It's sometimes lonely in the human sense, but God never leaves. He never moves. He waits on us to return to him each and every time.

He is with you as you obey his command.

I am a firm believer in living out the Gospel of Christ in every aspect as you have already read.

I pray first that you see that all grow in faith, wisdom, courage, and love.

Faith to trust God.
Wisdom to guide others.

Courage to choose Christ every day.
Love for all the way God loves.

    Second, I hope this inspires you share your story with others. God is a God of freedom. He does not want us to struggle alone. We are to live in communities that allow us to share freely with one another the life God wants us to live.

    Remember in everything that there is a " but God" at the end of the sentence, at the end of the day, and at the end of the week.

Welcome to my community!

Please continue to pray for me as I attempt to look like Christ and share his word with others.

Remember you are not perfect, but I pray that you decide to follow a God that is.

With all my Love!

Jasmine

bible bibliography

Holy Bible: English Standard Version. Wheaton, IL: Crossway Bibles, 2001. Print.

Holy Bible: Easy-to-read Version. Fort Worth, TX: World Bible Translation Center, 2006. Print.

Holy Bible: King James Version. Grand Rapids, MI: Zondervan, 2002. Print.

Holy Bible: New Living Translation. Wheaton, IL: Tyndale House, 1996. Print.

The Bible: New International Version. Colorado Springs, CO: International Bible Society, 1984. Print.

The Open Bible New American Standard Version. N.p.: Thomas Nelson, 2004. Print.

bibliography

"Bethel Sozo - Home." *Bethel Sozo - Home*. Bethel Sozo, 2013. Web.

Elevation Worship. *Kingdom Come*. Elevation Worship, 2010. MP3.

Lecrae. *Rebel vs. Gravity*. Theory Hazit, 2013. MP3.

Lecrae, J. R., Novel, Mathai, Swoope, Trip Lee, Thi'sl, Big K.R.I.T, Ashthon Jones, Pro, Sho Baraka, Andy Mineo, Tedashii, Damon Albarn, and Rudy Currence. *Gravity*. Lecrae. Reach, 2012. CD.

Mali Music. *The 2econd Coming*. Dedicated Music Group, 2009. CD.

McReynolds, Jonathan. *Life Music*. Entertainment One US LP, 2012. MP3.

Rath, Tom, and Marcus Buckingham. *StrengthsFinder 2.0*. New York: Gallup, 2007. Print.

Ronald Julian. *Vantage Point*. Ronald Julian, 2011. CD

ABOUT THE AUTHOR

Jasmine is from Monroe, La and a graduate of Xavier University of Louisiana. She is currently a student at Baylor University where is will earn her Doctorate of Philosophy is Sociology with a concentration in Applied Sociology. Her aspiration is to work at a Historically Black College or University in administration.

Currently, she works as a youth leader at Acts Church is Waco, TX. She loves high school students and seeing them grow as individuals and in Christ.

God is her refuge and strength and encouraging others is her past time.

Made in the USA
Charleston, SC
01 July 2015